T0224732

Media Innovations AR and VR

Elle Langer

Media Innovations AR and VR

Success Factors For The Development Of Experiences

 Springer

Elle Langer
Berlin, Germany

ISBN 978-3-662-66279-3   ISBN 978-3-662-66280-9   (eBook)
https://doi.org/10.1007/978-3-662-66280-9

This Springer imprint is published by the registered company Springer-Verlag GmbH, DE, part of Springer Nature.
The registered company address is: Heidelberger Platz 3, 14197 Berlin, Germany

Foreword

Virtual, mixed, and augmented reality (VR/MR/AR) are immersive media that take digitization in business and society to the next level. These media enable new forms of use. They simplify communication and production processes and thus the way we will learn, communicate and work in the future. This results in new challenges for companies and society.

Numerous applications for the immersive media AR, MR, and VR are currently being developed for areas such as education, marketing, health, and product manufacturing. However, uniform technical and legal standards as well as methods for workflows for the development of content and products are still missing for mass market maturity. Distribution channels through which larger user groups can use these media are also only just emerging.

In short, augmented reality, mixed reality, and virtual reality are media innovations that are in an early stage of development. These media still lack the relevance to enter the mass market.

This book by Elle Langer is a good example of a scientific work with a high practical relevance. The author analyzes the initial situation of the immersive media AR, MR, and VR in the context of media innovations in a scientifically sound manner. In doing so, she primarily considers the user and producer perspectives, which are relevant for the successful entry of media innovations into the market. The aim is to identify success factors that make it easier to develop products for AR, MR, and VR because they meet a user need and thus facilitate the production process and market entry.

For her analysis, Elle Langer draws from the fund of different scientific disciplines. Through her analysis of media and communication science, she expands the definition of "digital media" to include "immersive media" and places these in the context of media innovations. User experiences and emotions are an important success factor for the author, which she derives by means of theories from the cognitive, film, and social sciences.

The author systematically derives media-specific success factors for content development and the production process and condenses the results into action-guiding checklists.

These give the reader a good overview of the minimum standards needed to use modern innovation techniques to produce content for MR, VR, and AR that will lead to a high level of user acceptance and is truly wanted.

The checklists serve as a guideline for all those who produce immersive media content, and they are also a basis for the further development of IMMERSIVE STORYTELLING and IMMERSIVE MEDIA BUSINESS.

The basis for the findings in this book are 14 interviews, some of them lasting several hours, with experts from various industries who are already working with immersive media.

In addition, the author Elle Langer's many years of professional experience as a media producer and developer of media projects and media innovations comes into play, which she incorporates into her analysis. These increase the direct practical relevance.

Successfully implementing media innovations as projects depends on a variety of factors that go beyond the previously known criteria for media and digital products. In Elle Langer's scientific work, the author has highlighted the essential success factors from the user and producer perspectives.

The results presented in the book are presented and condensed in a very clear manner, resulting in a coherent structure of results throughout the book.

Overall, Elle Langer has succeeded in transferring the findings derived from the secondary literature and the expert survey very well, which are underpinned by a large number of practical examples. It is a pleasure to be introduced to the world of immersive media by the author.

Professor for Electronic Business at the   Thomas Schildhauer
University of Arts Berlin, Director
Institute of Electronic Business

Director Alexander von Humboldt
Institut für Internet und Gesellschaft
Berlin, Germany

Contents

About the Author

Elle Langer is an experienced and award-winning media producer and director for high-quality documentaries, non-fictional TV formats, and image films. Her projects cover cultural, edutainment, and social topics and are aimed at children, young people, and adults.

Since 2015, Elle Langer has focused on augmented, mixed, and virtual reality. For her, these media immediately have the potential for groundbreaking new forms of knowledge transfer and entertainment. At the same time, they are so new that too little is known about storytelling and production methods.

The author acquired profound knowledge about new media during her master's degree in "Leadership in Digital Communication/Innovation" (Universität der Künste/Universität St. Gallen), which she completed in 2017.

The success factors developed within the scope of this scientific work enable a scalable process. In the process, field-tested and scientifically based creative techniques for the production of VR and AR experiences are applied, such as design thinking and agile innovation management.

With her agency pimento formate, Elle Langer today designs VR and AR products for edutainment, marketing, and health. Her clients are media, creative agencies, museums, NGOs, and industrial companies looking for innovative media and communication products, including for AR and VR. User-centered, creative, and strategic-economic aspects play an important role.

In her workshops and lectures, Elle Langer presents the most important factors for success with the aim of introducing interested parties to the new media of augmented, mixed, and virtual reality.

As a co-founder and board member (2017–2020) of Virtual Reality Berlin-Brandenburg Association ., she is also actively involved in the expansion of the XR economy in Germany and Europe.

Elle Langer
Media Innovation Manager
Design Thinking Coach
Creative XR Producer
Member of the Board Virtual Reality Berlin-Brandenburg e.V.
pimento formate GmbH – Creative Tech Agency for XR Edutainment
e.langer@pimento-formate.de
978-3-662-60826-5.1. Genderhinweis

Introduction

1

Those who engage with immersive media today will secure their future viability.

Virtual Reality (VR) and Augmented and Mixed Reality (AR, MR) are new media technologies. They are subsumed under the notion of Extended Reality and are referred to in short form as XR[1] (cf. Sect. 3.2). They are said to change the way people communicate, work, live, learn and perceive reality (cf. Metzinger and Madary 2016, p. 2; Hildt 2011). By adding digital information and objects to a natural, real-physical environment, the immersive media[2] AR, MR and VR manipulate reality.

They open virtual spaces in real space people can enter. These virtual and virtually expanded spaces are empty, not yet modeled, like a cave, a new planet, or a construction site that needs to be designed and defined. It is in this area where the potential of immersive media technologies lies. The design and conquest of new spaces and the search for new experiences are part of human history and attract adventurers, business people, creatives and researchers.

---

[1] The terms virtual reality, augmented reality and mixed reality are defined in Sect. 3.2. For linguistic simplification, the short forms are used for the introduction: Virtual Reality as VR, Augmented Reality as AR, Mixed Reality as MR. This corresponds to the abbreviations commonly used in business and science. The term Extended Reality (XR) is rarely used in this book and only as a collective term (cf. Section 3.2).

[2] Since AR, MR and VR have an immersive effect on the user, they are also called immersive media or immersive media technologies (see Sect. 4.2.3).

E. Langer, *Media Innovations AR and VR*, https://doi.org/10.1007/978-3-662-66280-9_1

In an overpopulated world with saturated markets, overloaded advertising spaces and media overstimulation, immersive media offer the potential for new economic spaces, living spaces and places of entertainment and communication. Immersive media technologies make it possible to experience these parallel worlds.

1.1   Relevance of the Subject

After many years of development and ups and downs, the immersive media technologies augmented, mixed and virtual reality have established themselves. As future technologies – paired with artificial intelligence – they will further digitalize and connect our world. The hype surrounding them is over. In the next few years, they will be part of the industrial standard (cf. Buvat et al. 2018, pp. 6, 23). The Gartner Hype Cycle, an indicator for upcoming technology trends, already mentions the specific AR and VR trends in its innovation spectrum "immersive workspaces" and "augmented intelligence" (cf. Panetta 2019). Other specific applications – such as social virtual spaces exist already. The market for immersive media is considered a growth market worldwide. The global market potential of VR and AR is estimated at US$160 billion by 2023, with approximately 36.7 million VR headsets sold, according to a forecast by economic research firm IDC (see Shire 2019b). Interestingly, IDC analysts see the greatest growth potential for augmented and mixed reality, with a compound annual growth rate of over 140% (140.9%) through 2023. The reason for this is the increasing demand for AR glasses. The current market gap is expected to be filled by 31.9 million AR glasses and AR-enabled smartphones and tablets by 2023 (see Shire 2019a). After China and the US, Western Europe is the third-largest growth market (cf. Shire 2019b.).

And the XR industry is growing fast. An overview of the global growth of the industry and its differentiation in the individual industries is published by The Venture Fund in semi-annual reports (cf. The Venture Reality Fund 2019a). The Venture Fund is supported by investors who invest venture capital in start-ups for infrastructure, technology and content, primarily in the USA and China (cf. The Venture Reality Fund 2019b).

In the meantime, almost all branches of industry are interested in the new media technologies and are already working successfully with them.

In a US study, the majority (93%) of the 750 companies surveyed that work with VR/AR confirmed that the market is developing positively for them. For more than half of the respondents (57%), the decision to use immersive media had even boosted business. The respondents expect the breakthrough for AR in 2020, which is in line with the IDC assessment (cf. Hadwick 2019, p. 4).

A new globally growing industry is emerging, that of AR and VR producers. These are start-ups but also established companies that produce their XR products or do this as a service provider for others.

The focus is not on the B2C[3] mass market. Immersive media technologies are growing primarily in the B2B[4] niches of various industries. Companies are mainly interested in industry-specific AR and VR applications and invest in training, collaborative work, engineering and design tasks, and marketing activities (see Shire 2019a). VR and AR are therefore most commonly used in the education and training industry (55.8%), followed by architecture, engineering, construction trade (44.2%) and healthcare (42.3%) (cf. Hadwick, Alex 2019, p. 5). The figures on the use of XR media refer to US companies. There is no comparable survey for the respective industries in Germany or Europe as up to 2020. However, a study on the XR industry in the federal country of North Rhine-Westphalia (NRW) makes it clear that the greatest potential off AR and VR lies in the design and simulation sector (67%), followed by product presentations (62%) and training (60%) (cf. Zabel et al. 2019, p. 38). Further studies are currently in progress.

Many companies use VR simulations for several areas at once. Deutsche Bahn, for example, uses VR for training purposes to prepare employees for new train models (see Deutsche Bahn 2019b). For another division, the transport company visualizes train stations as VR simulations. The VR environments, which are created using construction drawings and planning data, are intended to support the implementation of elaborate construction projects. The same data and graphics are used to inform the public about the construction measures and to present the new station to them in advance in a VR simulation (cf. Deutsche Bahn 2019a). This example shows the economic potential of immersive technologies for companies. After all, once the expertise for implementing XR projects is available in the company, 3D models are increasingly easy to produce. And once these are in place, they can be used for multiple applications. In addition, immersive media technologies improve quality assurance, help to optimize work processes and make assembly procedures safer. In this way, immersive media also support digitization measures in companies and extend their value chain.

It is astonishing that according to a survey by the digital association Bitkom and the management consultancy Deloitte only 12% of the companies surveyed in Germany use AR and VR. 20% are still planning or discussing their use (cf. Esser and Gentemann 2019, p. 48).

The added value of immersive media as a teaching and training tool has already been confirmed many times in numerous studies. Therefore, AR and VR are already successfully used in education and health care.[5] In medicine, for example, as preparation for complicated surgical procedures, such as a spinal operation. Before the operation, the surgeon uses VR or AR to prepare himself for anatomical features of the patient's body.

---

[3] B2C is the abbreviation for business-to-consumer market, in which the offer of companies is directed at the consumer (cf. Krieger et al. 2018).

[4] B2B stands for business-to-business market. Here, the offer of companies is directed at other companies (cf. Kirchgeorg et al. 2018).

[5] A good overview of different application areas of VR and AR, e.g. in education and medicine, is offered by the Virtual Dimension Center in Fellbach (cf. VDC-Fellbach 2019).

The AR simulation then helps him to avoid spinal cord injuries during the operation as non-visible body parts are virtually visible to the surgeon (cf. Yoo et al. 2019).

It has been shown several times that VR simulations can be used successfully for therapeutic purposes. In patients with a fear of heights, a dementia disorder or after a stroke, motor and mental complaints could be notably alleviated (cf. Schnabel 2017; Mühlberger 2014, p. 149 f.; Freeman et al. 2018, pp. 625, 630 f.).

VR and AR content is also increasingly being produced for research purposes, e.g. for the reconstruction of historical places. Scientists can thus research the lifestyles and architecture of places that no longer exist and make them virtually accessible and experience-able for museum visitors (cf. Darmawiguna et al. 2019, p. 29 f.). Artists are working with scientists to develop novel digital artworks and art experiences (cf. Stark 2019, p. 105).

The large international digital corporations Facebook, Google, Microsoft, Apple and others recognized the potential of VR and AR years ago and are the market drivers (cf. Matney 2019, Zuckerberg 2015).

They invest in several market segments at once (cf. Weddeling 2017). Their goal is to expand their own ecosystem, consisting of VR glasses, VR platforms for their content, and VR and AR software to promote their products (cf. Bastian, Matthias August 15, 2017). In a joint project, the corporates Google, Microsoft, Mozilla, Apple and Facebook are developing a standard for WebVR and WebAR, with which AR and VR applications can be launched directly via all common internet browsers (cf. Bezmalinovic 2017). Even the world's largest online shop Amazon has entered the XR business and offers business customers tools with which they can build their own VR and AR content (cf. aws 2019).

The market is hot, including the B2C mass market. In Germany alone revenues of EUR 116 million were generated from VR content in 2018. That's 38% more than the year before. The VR games industry accounted for the largest share with EUR 62 million (revenue up 31%), followed by VR and 360° videos with EUR 43 million (revenue up 48%). For 2023, revenues of EUR 117 million are expected for 360° videos alone (cf. Ketterer 2019, p. 123).

In addition to games (VR 70%, AR 48%), the still small group of VR and AR users is mainly interested in 360° videos that make it possible to travel virtually to distant places (VR 49%) and to experience documentaries and movies (VR 42%) as well as music videos and concerts (15%) in a new way (cf. Esser and Gentemann 2019, p. 51).

High-quality and walk-in VR cinema productions (Cinematic VR[6]) are already being screened and awarded at international film festivals such as Venice or Toronto (cf. La Biennale Di Venezia 2019; FIVARS 2019). Access to these immersive cinematic experiences is possible through dedicated VR platforms with appropriate VR glasses. Despite the unique offerings, only one in five people in Germany (22%) have ever put on VR glasses. One in ten (10%) owns a pair of glasses (cf. Esser and Gentemann 2019, p. 49).

---

[6] Cinematic VR essentially covers the many approaches in which virtual reality content appropriates or applies film methods to deliver narrative experiences (see Unity 2019).

Content is king – and every technology needs application possibilities or use cases that provide users with a unique experience and added value in their everyday lives (cf. Chap. 5).

Content producers and scientists around the world are working to improve experiences for the 360° medium of VR. They create new narrative forms and dramaturgy so that the user identifies with the protagonists – either avatars[7] or real people – in the virtual environment. For the VR film "Wolves in the Wall" (Emmy Award 2019), for example, new interaction possibilities were developed that are built into the story (see Future of Storytelling, October 02, 2019). It is an approach to new audiovisual experiences and the search for the best use cases that users can only experience with XR.

The private media groups and public broadcasters have also recognized immersive media as a new playout channel. They produce content for VR, AR or 360° documentaries for journalistic and educational purposes (cf. WDR 2019a, b). Private media groups invest in start-ups and thus build new business fields for XR entertainment (cf. Pauker 2019) as do streaming services like Netflix or Deutsche Telekom: They produce 360° music concerts, travel experiences and series for their own VR platforms (cf. Netflix 2016; Reinhard 2019). Platforms such as Facebook and others tend to focus on VR and AR games (cf. Heath 2019).

The game Pokémon Go is an important pioneer for AR technology in 2016. However, almost unnoticed AR technology is being expanded on social network platforms such as Snapchat and Instagram. They offer their users graphical layers to manipulate their selfies and their surroundings. In this way users make their AR content. For the expansion of its own AR platform, Snapchat took on a billion US dollars in debt, but thanks to its AR offering, it can increase its user numbers and thus its revenue in 2019 (cf. Dang 2019). This shows that an easy, playful access via smartphone – coupled with added value for the user – lowers the barrier to entry into AR.

A good example of user-added value is the AR app of the furniture store IKEA. It supports customers in making purchasing decisions by virtually integrating furniture into the room with the help of the AR app. To make this possible, the furniture store is breaking new ground and in 2017 entered into a cooperation with the software and hardware manufacturer Apple, which is introducing its ARKit technology with this collaboration (cf. Miller 2019).

The innovative power of VR and AR makes it clear that companies are willing to enter into unusual collaborations in order to establish themselves in the AR and VR market at an early stage through user-relevant applications. The goal is to use AR and VR to build new customer relationships and gain user data that can be used to offer further products and services (cf. Esser et al. 2016, p. 51).

The cross-industry activities and the variety of possible applications with AR and VR are changing the value chain for all market participants. This softens the boundaries

---

[7] Avatar is the term for a non-real, computer-based on-screen figure of a user in virtual worlds and encounters such as in online role-playing games or chats (cf. Kollmann 2018).

between industries. This is also confirmed by the Deloitte-Bitkom study (2017), which points out that the activities of large companies and platform operators drive out small players of the market. This particularly affects media producers whose market segment is content production (cf. Esser et al. 2016, p. 52).

These content producers are ready to offer their creative knowledge and technical services worldwide. But producing content for VR and AR is complex, expensive and risky. The industry, therefore, implements its XR projects primarily as research and development projects. In this way they become better acquainted with immersive media and can assess the possibilities they offer better (cf. Buvat et al. 2018, p. 8). This enables these companies to build up their own competencies as content producers.

The low willingness to invest in content or XR start-ups can also be observed among German investors as revenues from digital products and services such as e-commerce are still more likely (cf. Lennartz 2019, pp. 7, 14). There is a lack of empirical values and measurable success factors with which capital providers can better assess the risk when investing in XR start-ups and XR technology.

Poor financing options for XR content and applications are also slowing down market development. This points to an economic imbalance in the XR market as software and hardware always require an offering of application and content.

Media producers find themselves in the middle of this imbalance. They produce creative and informative films and games as cultural and economic goods. Most of them are SMEs (small and medium-sized enterprises) or sole proprietorships and are based in the creative industries (cf. Sect. 6.1). So far, however, only a small number of media producers produce content and products for AR and VR.

They are opposed by large international corporations and other market players who are building up their own competencies in immersive media technologies.

This situation presents media producers in particular with the challenge of defining their role in the new market. They must develop new forms of audiovisual information and entertainment delivery (cf. Esser et al. 2016, p. 49 f.). This also means changing previous approaches to product development and - by opening up to other industries - facing new economic framework conditions so that they can remain innovative and fit for the future.

Both companies and media producers could benefit from each other's expertise.

This book is intended to help media producers and companies interested in immersive media technologies to benefit from the experiences of many producers to date. It provides them with scientifically proven success factors as a minimum requirement for VR and AR content production to avoid mistakes and higher costs. It also gives examples that show why it is helpful to collaborate with other industries.

Literature

AWS (2019): Amazon Sumerian; URL: https://aws.amazon.com/de/sumerian/, Abruf 06.10.2019.

Bezmalinovic, Tamislav (06.07.2017): Virtual Reality: Apple tritt WebVR-Initiative, bei, MIXED Online Magazin; URL: https://mixed.de/virtual-reality-apple-tritt-webvr-initiative-bei/, Abruf 09.10.2019.

Buvat, Jerome et al. (07.09.2018): AR and VR in Operations Report, Capgemini Research Institut; URL: https://www.capgemini.com/de-de/resources/augmented-reality-virtual-reality-unternehmen-studie/?utm_source=pr&utm_medium=referral&utm_content=none_countryor-ganic_link_report_none&utm_campaign=disruptdigital_ri_ar-vr, Abruf 05.10.2019.

Dang, Sheila (06.08.2019): Snap to raise $1 billion to invest in AR, possible acquisitions, Reuters; URL: https://www.reuters.com/article/us-snap-convertible-notes/snap-to-raise-1-billion-to-invest-in-ar-possible-acquisitions-idUSKCN1UW1OB, Abruf: 09.10.2019.

Darmawiguna, Mahendra et al. (2019): Bali Temple VR: The Virtual Reality Based Application for the Digitalization of Balinese Temples in: Kultur und Informatik: Virtual History and Augmented Present, Carsten Busch, Christian Kassung, Jürgen Sieck (Hrsg.), Verlag Werner Hülsbusch, Glückstadt, S. 29–39.

Deutsche Bahn (2019a): Another World VR – Gamingexperten für die Öffentlichkeitsarbeit; URL: https://www.deutschebahn.com/de/Digitalisierung/startups/db_startups/AnotherWorld-VR-3528678, Abruf 29.9.2019.

Deutsche Bahn, (2019b): „Augmented Education" bringt Züge und Weichen ins Klassenzimmer, Digitalisierung, Immersive Technologien; URL: https://www.deutschebahn.com/de/Digitalisierung/technologie/Neue-Technologien/Immersive-Technologien-3374488, Abruf 29.09.2019.

Esser, Ralf; Böhm, Claus; Lutter, Tim (2016): Zukunft der Consumer Technology- Bitkom e. V.: Berlin; URL: https://www.bitkom.org/sites/default/files/file/import/160831-CT-Studie-2016-online.pdf, Abruf 09.10.2019.

Esser, Ralf; Gentemann, Lukas (2019): Zukunft der Consumer Technologie-2019, Marktentwicklung, Trends, Mediennutzung, Technologien, Geschäftsmodelle; Bitkom Deloitte (Hrsg.), URL: https://www.bitkom.org/sites/default/files/2019-09/190903_ct_studie_2019_online.pdf, Abruf 06.10.2019.

FIVARS (2019): Festival of International Virtual and Augmented Reality Stories; URL: https://fivars.net/, Abruf 089.10.2019.

Freeman, D.; Haselton, P. et al. (2018): Automated psychological therapy using immersive virtual reality for treatment of fear of heights: a single-blind, parallel-group, randomised controlled trial, Lancet Psychiatry 2018;5: S. 625–632, Published Online 11.07. 2018; URL: https://www.thelancet.com/action/showPdf?pii=S2215-0366%2818%2930226-8, Abruf 29.09.2019.

Future of Storytelling (02.10.2019): Q&A with Pete Billington of Emmy Award–Winning Fable Studio; URL: https://medium.com/future-of-storytelling/q-a-with-pete-billington-of-emmy-award-winning-fable-studio-164ff13c00df, Abruf 04.10.2019.

Hadwick, Alex (2019): XR Industry Insight Report 2019-2020; URL: https://eloqua.vr-intelligence.com/LP=25319, Abruf 29.09.2019.

Heath, Alex (10.07.2019): Next on Facebook's Shopping List: Acquisitions to Beef Up Gaming, The Information; URL: https://www.theinformation.com/articles/next-on-facebooks-shopping-list-acquisitions-to-beef-up-gaming, Abruf 09.10.2019.

Ketterer, Simeon (2019): German Entertainment and Media Outlook 2019 – 2023, PWC Deutschland GEMO, URL: https://www.pwc.de/de/technologie-medien-und-telekommunikation/german-entertainment-and-media-outlook-2019-2023.html, Abruf 30.10.2019.

Kirchgeorg, Manfred et al. (2018) Stichwort: B2B, Gabler Wirtschaftslexikon (Hrsg.), Springer Gabler Verlag; URL: https://wirtschaftslexikon.gabler.de/definition/business-business-markt-28155/version-251791, Abruf 09.10.2019.

Kollmann, Tobias (2018) Stichwort: Avatar, Gabler Wirtschaftslexikon (Hrsg.), Springer Gabler Verlag; URL: https://wirtschaftslexikon.gabler.de/definition/avatar-31903/version-255451, Abruf 05.10.2019.

Krieger, Winfried et al. (2018) Stichwort: B2C, Gabler Wirtschaftslexikon (Hrsg.), Springer Gabler Verlag; URL: https://wirtschaftslexikon.gabler.de/definition/business-consumer-markt-30024/version-253618, Abruf 09.10.2019.

La Biennale Di Venezia (2019): Venice Virtual Reality; URL: https://www.labiennale.org/en/cinema/2019/venice-vr, Abruf 09.10.2019.

Lennartz, Peter (2019): Start-ups, Aiming High. Das Start-up-Barometer 2018 Midterm, Ernst and Young Research; URL: https://www.ey.com/Publication/vwLUAssets/ey-start-up-barometer-deutschland-januar-2019/%24FILE/ey-start-up-barometer-deutschland-januar-2019.pdf, Abruf am 09.10.2019.

Matney, Lucas (04.02.2019): Facebook mulled multi billion acquisition of unity claims, techcrunch; URL: https://techcrunch.com/2019/02/13/facebook-mulled-multi-billion-dollar-acquisition-of-unity-book-claims/, Abruf 06.10.2019.

Metzinger, T.; Hildt, E. (2011): Cognitive enhancement, in The Oxford Handbook of Neuroethics, eds J. Illes and B. J. Sahakian; Oxford, NY: Oxford University Press; Oxford Library of Psychology, S. 245–264.

Metzinger, Thomas; Madary, Michael (19.02.2016): Real Virtuality: A Code of Ethical Conduct. Recommendations for Good Scientific Practice and the Consumers of VR Technology, Volume 3 Article 3; in Frontiers in Robotics and AI; URL: http://journal.frontiersin.org/article/10.3389/frobt.2016.00003/full, Abruf am 09.10.2019.

Miller, Chance (23.09.2019): IKEA's ARKit furniture app ‚Place' overhauled with new interface, room sets, more; on 9to5mac; URL: https://9to5mac.com/2019/09/23/ikea-place-ios-ar-app/, Abruf 05.10.2019.

Mühlberger, Andreas (2014): Virtuelle Realität in der Klinischen Emotions- und Psychotherapieforschung, In: Jeschke, Sabine; Kobbelt, Leif; Dröge, Alicia (Hrsg.): Exploring Virtuality, Wiesbaden: Springer Fachmedien, S. 149–161.

Netflix (04.08.2016): The Stranger Things Trailer; YouTube; URL: https://www.youtube.com/watch?v=yg29RvYNSDQ, Abruf 06.10.2019.

Panetta, Kasey (29.08.2019): 5 Trends Appear on the Gartner Hype Cycle for Emerging Technologies; URL: https://www.gartner.com/smarterwithgartner/5-trends-appear-on-the-gartner-hype-cycle-for-emerging-technologies-2019, Abruf 20190926.

Pauker, Manuela (20.5.2019): Pro7Sat1 investiert in Virtual-Reality-Entertainment, Werben und Verlaufen Online; URL: https://www.wuv.de/medien/prosiebensat_1_investiert_in_virtual_reality_entertainment, Abruf 04.10.2019.

Reinhard, Malte (05.09.2019): Magenta Virtual Reality: Deutsche Telekom setzt neue Maßstäbe; Telekom, URL: https://www.telekom.de/zuhause/entertainment/musik-und-videos/virtual-reality, Abruf 09.10.2019.

Schnabel, Susanne (14.09.2017): Virtual Reality soll Demenzkranken helfen; URL: http://www1.wdr.de/wissen/mensch/datenbrille-demenz-virtual-reality-demenz-100.html, Abruf am 19.10.2019 (Verfügbar bis 17.09.2022).

Shire, Michael (28.03.2019a): Augmented Reality and Virtual Reality Headsets Poised for Significant Growth, According to IDC; URL: https://www.idc.com/getdoc.jsp?containerId=prUS44966319, Abruf 08.10.2019.

Shire, Michael (04.06.2019b): Commercial and Public Sector Investments Will Drive Worldwide AR/VR Spending to $160 Billion in 2023, According to a New IDC Spending Guide; URL: https://www.idc.com/getdoc.jsp?containerId=prUS45123819, Abruf 29.9.2019.

Stark, Maja (2019): The AURORA School: School for Artists: Artistic Augmented Reality Applications in Cooperation with the Independent Arts & Culture Scene in Berlin: in Kultur und Informatik: Virtual History and Augmented Present; Carsten Busch, Christian Kassung, Jürgen Sieck (Hrsg.), Verlag Werner Hülsbusch, Glückstadt, S. 105–137.

The Venture Reality Fund (2019a): Industry Landscape; URL: http://www.thevrfund.com/resources/industry-landscape/, Abruf 29.09.2019.

The Venture Reality Fund (2019b): Who are we – XR meets AI; URL: http://www.thevrfund.com/about-us/, Abruf 5.10.2019.

Unity (2019: What is AR, VR, MR, XR, 360? Stichwort Cinematic VR; Unity Glossary; URL: https://unity3d.com/what-is-xr-glossary, Abruf 08.10.2019.

VDC-fellbach (2019): Virtual Reality für Therapie und Diagnose; VDC-Wissen; URL: https://www.vdc-fellbach.de/wissen/anwendungsfelder/therapie-und-diagnose/, Abruf 09.10.2019.

Yoo, J.S., Patel, D.S., Hrynewycz, N.M. et al. (12.06.2019): The utility of virtual reality and augmented reality in spine surgery, Vol 7, (September 2019): Annals of Translational Medicine, in "Current Trends and Advancements in Spine Surgery"; URL: http://atm.amegroups.com/article/view/26784/html, Download: http://atm.amegroups.com/article/view/26784/24323, Abruf 05.10.2019.

WDR (2019a): Glückauf; URL: https://glueckauf.wdr.de/, Abruf 06.10.2019.

WDR (2019b): Zeitkapsel; URL: https://zeitkapsel.wdr.de/, Abruf 06.10.2019.

Weddeling, Britta (24.05.2017): Googles Tagträume, Kolumne Future Lab, Handelsblatt; URL: http://www.handelsblatt.com/my/unternehmen/it-medien/kolumne-future-lab-googles-tagtraeume/19844272.html, Abruf am 09.10.2019.

Zabel, Christian; Heisenberg G.; Telkmann V. (2019): XR in NRW Potenziale und Bedarfe der nordrhein-westfälischen Virtual, Mixed und Augmented Reality-Branche Mediennetzwerk.NRW (Hrsg.); URL: https://medien.nrw.de/wp-content/uploads/2019/06/XR-Studie-NRW-2019.pdf, Abruf 05.10.2019.

Zuckerberg, Mark (22.06.2015) Mark's Vision; URL: https://de.scribd.com/document/399594551/2015-06-22-MARK-S-VISION#from_embed, Abruf 06.10.2019.

Methods

2

Knowing the characteristics of XR media technologies helps in product development.

The methodological approach chosen is the expert interview, which can provide conclusions about success factors employing a qualitative content analysis. Qualitative content analysis is an exploratory research method that examines fixed data, such as writing, text or images through categorization and coding. The systematic extraction of textual information based on evaluation criteria can provide clues to the research question (cf. Gläser and Laudel 2010, p. 48 f.).

The experts in this work are producers who have specialist knowledge. The experts are already experienced in the production of AR and VR applications (cf. Gläser and Laudel 2010, p. 12 f.). They build a focus group. The expert interview is based on the secondary analysis of media-relevant aspects of AR and VR in Sections 3.1 to 6.2.

2.1 Expert Interviews

The expert statements are analyzed, sorted and summarized according to defined categories. The categories are formed in three steps. In the first step, the three categories of **content**, **user** and **economy** are identified in connection with the concept of media (cf. Sects. 3.6.2, 4.2.3 and 4.3). In the second step, the consideration of user needs in Chap. 5 specifies the category "user" concerning the user experience in AR and VR applications. The third step integrates the **producer level** and thus the initial situation and **learnings** of the producers (cf. Table 2.1).

© The Author(s), under exclusive license to Springer-Verlag GmbH, DE, part of
Springer Nature 2023
E. Langer, *Media Innovations AR and VR*,
https://doi.org/10.1007/978-3-662-66280-9_2

Table 2.1 Brief overview of the categories

Categories	Subcategories
Content	Media format, story, three-dimensionality space and content, Interaction and communication, linking space and content
Users	User experience of media use, three-dimensional spatial experience, Physical experience, interaction and communication experience
Economics	Production and production method, team Economic and structural framework conditions
Producer	Initial situation Motivation
Learnings	Special experiences, Findings and assessments

The five categories of content, user, economy, producer and learning form the basis of the expert interview, which was conducted using an interview guide. The five categories are subdivided into further subcategories for this purpose (cf. Section 6.2).

The interviews were conducted in person, recorded and transcribed according to simple scientific transcription rules, and the language was smoothed (cf. Dresing and Pehl 2018, p. 20 f.). The content analysis was carried out by reducing the text and assigning the text passages to four success factors (cf. Appendix 3 and 4). The evaluation criteria of the success factors are presented in short form (cf. Appendix 3):

Success factor 1: This has worked well or is standardized.

Success factor 2: This worked particularly well and is something special.

Success factor 3: This was new or surprised the producer.

Success factor 4: This did not work at all or is a risk.

According to the extraction rule, the text passages are underlined or highlighted in bold. Time codes and coding are used to identify the producers and assign them to the evaluation (cf. Gläser, Gläser and Laudel 2010, pp. 199–204). The results of the interviews are summarized and interpreted in Chap. 7. These form the success factors for content production on the user and producer level and are summarized as checklists.[1] They serve as a guide for the scalable production of content for AR and VR applications.[2]

2.1.1   Selection of experts

The experts are primarily based in the media industry, which is part of the creative industries (cf. Section 6.1). Experts from other sectors are also consulted. The aim is to gather as broad a spectrum of knowledge as possible in order to identify the different experiences as success factors. The experts are selected according to the following criteria:

---

[1] The checklists provide an overview of the success factors in Annex 4.

[2] Questions about the research design, interview guide, and interviews can be emailed directly to the author, Elle Langer.

The experts have experience in the production of AR or VR applications.

The experts produce AR or VR products for entertainment purposes or knowledge transfer.

The experts work in companies of different sizes and at different locations in Germany.

The experts are active in various industries.

According to these criteria, 14 experts from nine companies and organizations were selected, including four companies from the media industry, one engine manufacturer, one concert promoter, one company each from the entertainment sector, the training sector and a research institution. They represent eight projects. These include three augmented reality projects, four virtual reality projects and one mixed reality project (cf. Table 2.2).

Table 2.2 Overview of experts

	Industry	Project	Description
A)	**Media industry**		
1	**WDR** **Thomas Hallet** Project manager and head of the innovation department	Project: "360Dom. de" Virtual reality project CGI production With 360° videos	Thomas Hallet initiated and supervised the entire project with five WDR colleagues and external employees. In the VR application users experience the Cologne cathedral through content offerings such as 360° videos, flights through the cathedral and other interaction options.
2	**UFA lab** **Floris ash** Story creation **Daniel Brückner** Project management	Project: "Gateway to infinity" Virtual reality project CGI and human body reconstruction	Daniel Brückner and Floris Asche wrote the story and implemented it dramaturgically and in terms of content. In the sci-fi scenario, the user stands on a rock in front of a cave entrance and watches two real actors guarding the gate to eternity. The user can get close to the actors.
3	**UFA serial** **Drama** **Frank Govaere** CGI creation **Ernst Feiler** Production manager UFA	with two actors, Walk-in movie	As head of production at UFA, Ernst Feiler is interested in building up a technical infrastructure for novel technologies and integrating them into UFA's workflow. Frank Govaere is a visual and special effects (VFX) expert at UFA and was responsible for VR space design.
4	**Miriquidi film** Michael Geidel Managing director and project manager AR contents	Project: "Pastors' children" Augmented reality project for Museum knowledge transfer	Michael Geidel is the managing director and produces film and TV movies, transmedia projects, gaming and VR films. The company is based in Munich, Leipzig and Potsdam. The AR project Pfarrerskinder (Pastors' Children) was developed as a supplement to the travelling exhibition as part of the Reformation anniversary for "Luther Year 2017".

(continued)

Table 2.2 (continued)

	Industry	Project	Description
B)	**Holodeck/entertainment**		
5	**EXIT VR** **Sven Häberlein** Executive director, Project manager creation	Project: "Huxley" Virtual reality Project as Location-based Escape room Game	Sven Häberlein is co-founder of the start-up exit VR, which operates an escape room. Groups of players go through a VR application in teams and have to try to get out of the room using playful elements.
6	**Illusion walk** **Jim Rüggeberg** Managing director **Andrea Heuck** Project manager science	Project: "Immersive desk" VR CGI production For training and entertainment	Jim Rüggeberg and his brother Julien developed a walk-through holodeck in 2013. In the VR goggles the user enters an elevator to an off-shore platform. Up there he makes repairs. The holodeck was developed for training and games and can integrate any content, such as walk-in showrooms or films.
C)	**Concert hall**		
7	**Concert house** **Berlin** **Albrecht Sensch** Project manager technology **Annette Thoma** Project manager music	Project: "Concert house plus" AR app for innovative knowledge transfer Classical music	The Berlin Konzerthaus hosts 600 classical music concerts a year. The AR project "Konzerthaus plus" is part of the project "das Virtuelle Konzerthaus". This project intends to communicate classical music in a new way. Albrecht Sensch is responsible for the implementation as technical director. Annette Thoma is responsible for the musicological side.
D)	**Science**		
8	**Cologne games** **lab** **Dr. Björn** **Bartholdy** Co-director and head of games research **Katharina** **Tillmanns** VR & AR games research and research manager HisToGo	Project: "HisToGo" AR app A game for the knowledge transfer of historical contents	Dr. Björn Bartholdy is co-director of the Cologne games lab, which is located at the TH Köln. He is responsible, among other things, for the development of new research projects. The research project "HisToGo" is an AR game for historical knowledge transfer. The research director is Katharina Tillmanns.
E)	**Industry**		
9	**Rolls Royce** **Dr. Marius** **Swoboda** Project manager	Product: Development Mixed reality CAVE with Interactive CGI production	To improve product development, the British engine manufacturer rolls Royce has built a CAVE that allows engineers to work collaboratively in teams and at different locations. Dr. Marius Swoboda, as head of rolls Royce's internal department for human-machine design research, developed the project together with the University of Cottbus and installed it at rolls Royce.

Overview of the producers for the expert interviews (Own representation)

Literature

Gläser, Jochen; Laudel, Grit (2010): Experteninterview und qualitative Inhaltsanalyse als Instrument rekonstruierender Untersuchungen, 4. Auflage, Wiesbaden: VS Verlag für Sozialwissenschaften.

Dresing, Thorsten; Pehl, Thorsten (2018): Praxisbuch Interview, Transkription & Analyse, 8. Auflage, Eigenverlag: Marburg. URL: http://www.audiotranskription.de/download/praxisbuch_transkription.pdf?q=Praxisbuch-Transkription.pdf, Abruf am 31.10.2019.

Clarification of Terms

3

Knowing the characteristics of XR media technologies helps in product development.

In this chapter relevant definitions of virtual and augmented reality and their identifying characteristics are presented. The goal is to establish comparability based on the characteristics and to derive a working definition. Historical aspects are included to clarify the concepts behind augmented and virtual reality. This approach shows that the definitions of augmented and virtual reality are influenced by the stages of technological development and research perspective, and thus will continue to evolve and change. The similarity characteristics of augmented and virtual reality are derived into a working definition. This is based on the assumption that augmented and virtual reality should be considered as media based on their characteristics, and this new way of looking at them can provide clues to potential success factors for content production for augmented and virtual reality media innovations.

3.1 Historical Excursus

As things stand today, the origins of virtual, mixed and augmented reality have two distinct strands of development: One in media and art history and the other in technology. The creation of virtual spaces is part of media development, whose large-scale paintings in space have an immersive effect on the viewer, giving him a sensory experience and allowing him to immerse himself in them (cf. Grau 2001, p. 43 f.). The contemplation of a representation of nature in a 360° image led Alexander von Humboldt to believe that it could "[…] almost replace the wandering through diverse climates. Circular paintings accomplish more than stagecraft, because the viewer as if spellbound in a magic circle and removed from all disturbing reality, imagines himself surrounded by alien nature itself." (Humboldt, Alexander 1993, p. 79 f.; quoted from Grau 2001, p. 48). Cultural and media history speaks of illusion creation, which Oliver Grau and other cultural and media historians place in the current reference of digitalized worlds. According to Grau, illusion creation seems to be a central driver for the development of new media with technologies to invent ever new tools and create new forms of content representation. In this context the term "illusion" stands for sensory illusion or the wishful thinking of something (cf. Scholze-Stubenrecht et al. 2006, p. 523). The history of media and culture is full of examples. There are the panoramic images in the illusion spaces of the baroque, mechanical theatre stage techniques that created new worlds or the motion sequence of photographic frames that create the illusion of a realistic world in the viewer. An example is offered by the Lumière brothers' film screening in Paris where a train virtually enters the café on a screen, which is continued today in 360° dome cinemas or computer-generated and augmented virtual spaces (cf. Grau 2001, pp. 43, 47, 48; Hickethier 2012, p. 42). In terms of media and cultural history, augmented, mixed and virtual reality continue this development.

The technological development thread of virtual and augmented reality has its origins in the development of human-machine interfaces, the beginning of which is associated with the American computer graphics scientist Ivan Sutherland (cf. Dörner et al. 2013, p. 19). In 1961, Sutherland laid the foundation for interactive computer-generated two-dimensional graphic representations (cf. Kayyali, M. Saleh 30.05.2012, TC 5:00–6:45). Building on this, Sutherland developed the visionary idea of a data helmet, a so-called head-mounted display (HMD for short), for a graphical extension of the real physical environment. Sutherland combines the HMD with auditory and haptic stimuli that enable the wearer to experience a virtual environment, which he describes as follows: "The ultimate display would […] be a room within which the computer can control the existence of matter. […] Handcuffs displayed in such a room would be confining, and a bullet displayed in such a room would be fatal. With appropriate programming such a display could literally be the Wonderland into which Alice walked." (Sutherland 1965, pp. 506–508).

Since 1963, an international scene of engineers, computer graphic designers, and visionaries has been developing, coming together in organizations[1] such as IEEE, SIGGRAPH, or SPIE and publishing all the papers presented at their conferences. As of

---

[1] This overview shows the most important organizations and scientific sources for technological literature on augmented, mixed and virtual reality: MIT, Massachusetts Institute of Technology, URL: http://mitpressjournals.org, IEEE, Institute of Electrical and Electronics Engineers, URL: www.ieee.org, SIGGRAPH, Association for Computering Machinery, URL: http://www.siggraph.org/, SPIE, The International Society for Optics and Photonics, URL: https://spie.org/?SSO=1

retrieval on October 30, 2019, there were over 420 million publications in various contexts on IEEE's Library Platform under the term virtual reality, and over 85 million under augmented reality (cf. IEEE Library search terms 30.10.2019). The library grows by several thousand publications within weeks. The source material for virtual and augmented reality from a technological perspective documents the importance of media technology in science and industry. At the same time, the historical excursus makes clear that virtual and augmented reality are more than technologies. This is demonstrated by the growing number of international AR and VR trade fairs and conferences, such as Augmented World Expo (AWE), Laval Virtual, VR Days Europe, and many others, where content applications are presented alongside technology (cf. AWE 16.10.2019; Laval Virtual 16.10.2019; VR Days Europe 30.10.2019).

This book, therefore, sets out to look at virtual and augmented reality from a media perspective. The clarification of terms is an important basis for this and the prerequisite for the analysis of success factors of content production for innovative content and applications.

3.2   Definitions

The following definitions introduce the concepts of virtual, augmented and mixed reality. The basis of the definition clarification are the definitions commonly used in science and those derived from their historical context because the earlier definitions already contain the ideas of virtual, augmented and mixed reality and their possibilities. For better comprehensibility some sources are cited in the original.

The focus of the clarification of terms is on the specific characteristics of augmented, mixed and virtual reality. The focus is on identifying content and user-specific features that enable a media reference.

Technological definitions play a subordinate role. They are only described in order to understand the technical implementation.

The terms innovation and media innovation are defined in Sects. 4.3 and 4.4.

In recent years, in addition to the terms augmented, mixed and virtual reality, the term extended reality, abbreviated XR, established itself. Historically, its origin is linked to a product name. In the meantime, the term XR has gained international acceptance as a collective term for augmented, virtual and mixed reality. It was introduced on May 30 at the Augmented World Expo (AWE) in Santa Clara and serves as a linguistic simplification as it encompasses all forms of virtual and real realities (cf. Mann et al. 08.04.2018).

For better understanding and differentiation of the features, the terms augmented reality, mixed reality and virtual reality are used in this book.

3.3   Definition of Virtual Reality

The term virtual reality is composed of the English words virtual and reality. The German equivalent is virtuelle Realität (cf. Messinger et al. 1997, pp. 1321, 962). Virtual reality is a computer-generated simulation of reality. The French adjective – virtuelle – establishes the cultural-historical context to reality and describes the seemingly existent (cf. Scholze-Stubenrecht et al. 2006, p. 1088).

3.3.1   Characteristics of Virtual Reality

In scientific publications of the 1990s scientists speak of the virtual environment, short-form (VE), by which they mean the artificial graphic environment (cf. Azuma 1997, p. 2). In this book, the now common abbreviated form VR is used. From a technology perspective there are other relevant descriptions, such as that of Carolina Cruz-Neira. She is considered a pioneer in the study of virtual environments. For the 1993 SIGGRAPH conference, she offered a summary of the understanding of VR at the time: "Virtual Reality refers to immersive, interactive, multi-sensory, viewer-centered, three-dimensional computer-generated environments and the combination of technologies required to build these environments." (Cruz-Neira, Carolina 1993; cited in Dörner et al. 2013, p. 13).

Cruz-Neira describes VR as an immersive, interactive, three-dimensional, multisensory computer-generated environment that allows this environment to emerge through the combination of further technologies. The quote comes from Ralf Dörner's scientific textbook on AR and VR (cf. Dörner et al. 2013, p. 13). Cruz-Neira's explanation is supplemented there with Steve Bryson's definition. "Virtual Reality (VR) refers to the use of three-dimensional displays and interaction devices to explore real-time computer-generated environments." (Bryson, Steve 1993, cited in Dörner et al. 2013, p. 13).

In summary VR is an immersive, multisensory, and user-centered experience in a three-dimensional computer-generated environment composed of a combination of multiple technologies in which the user interacts in real-time. One feature is stepping into the virtual space by teleporting the user from one space to another without actually moving through it. Teleportation describes the transfer of people and objects from one place to another without having to pass through rooms. This is done by changing the virtual environment, for example by using an interaction point or optically changing to another 360° environment. In this process the user's sensory perceptions are focused on the computer-generated and media-based representations (cf. Dörner et al. 2013, pp. 17, 176).

A key feature of virtual reality is immersion, a media-generated state that gives the user a feeling of physical or psychological immersion in a media environment. The stimuli of the real-physical[2] world are no longer perceived. The user feels present in the virtual environment (cf. Craig 2013, p. 22; Sadowski and Stanney 2002, pp. 791–806; Mühlberger 2014, p. 152).

VR pioneer Jaron Lanier has described a total of 52 different definitions for VR in his book "Dawn of a New Era" (Anbruch einer neuen Zeit). They are not scientifically representative but illustrate the entire spectrum of VR in its multiple dimensionalities, which also takes into account a person's experience with and in VR. A technology in which internal data and algorithms are intelligible as transformations of real-time, point-of-view human experiences and thus inspire curiosity to look under the hood. (Lanier 2018, p. 242).

3.3.2 Technical Characteristics

Since a VR system is highly complex, the following application examples are outlined in simplified form. Technical details are not relevant to this book.

For a simulation in virtual reality, VR systems are used, which consist of a combination of computer hardware, software, sensors and displays.

The hardware and software elements are used to create computer-generated worlds (virtual reality) in which interactions with other media are possible (cf. Dörner et al. 2013, p. 7). The VR system is installed stationary in a real physical space. Through a tracking system consisting of sensors, cameras or other optical image recognition, the user's body movements and viewing directions in space are detected in real-time and synchronized with the virtual representation (cf. Grimm et al. 2013, pp. 109, 170). VR systems are integrated, for example, in-game consoles or holodecks. A holodeck is a three-dimensional (3D) walkable virtual space in which virtual or real objects or people can appear. The name traces back to the holodeck … which creates an artificial world around people for recreational, vocational or educational purposes. (cf. Stoppe 2016, p. 5). In a real holodeck, users wear a head-mounted display (HMD) or VR goggles with headphones, through which they experience the virtual environment.

The content for VR applications consists of audiovisual media formats, such as 3D graphics, animations, or 360° videos, which are supplemented by haptic or olfactory elements (cf. Grimm et al. 2013, p. 154). Formats are described in the media industry as creative media content such as games, TV series, magazine shows or magazines. Conceptually, formats provide the creative framework for the content (cf. Deuerling 2015, p. 31 f.; Fröhlich 2008, p. 152). In differentiation, the term media format is used here as a technological shell for media content. Formats are, for example, 360° videos that

---

[2] The term real-physical world or environment in this book refers to the naturally existing environment or world that is not manipulated by artificial digital elements. The opposite is the computer generated artificial (virtual) world, in its gradations of virtuality. This approach intends to distinguish the different concepts of virtuality.

reproduce realistic representations of a real-physical environment. They are filmed with a camera system consisting of several camera lenses, which record the environment in a 360° perspective. The user can view the filmed environment with the VR glasses in an all-round view.

3.3.3 VR Applications for Volumetric Images

Real physical persons or objects can now be integrated into a virtual 3D environment. To do this, the persons or objects are recorded from all directions in a volumetric studio (360° studio) by a recording system – consisting of up to 100 video cameras and, if necessary, additional depth sensors – and 3D scans of them are produced. This is possible in the 360° studio developed by Microsoft in London (cf. Janssen 2018, p. 114; Microsoft 2019).

The volumetric studio in Potsdam Babelsberg, developed by the Fraunhofer Heinrich Hertz Institute, produces differently (cf. Schreer et al. 2019). In the circular and single-walled studio real people are recorded with 32 cameras (16 camera pairs) and converted into 3D models. The technology is called 3D human body reconstruction (3D-HBR). The cameras, which have a very high resolution (4 k × 5 k), enable the exact reconstruction of a human being, his movements, facial expressions, hair and clothing. A data volume of 1.6 TB/min is generated in the process. The video data is converted to point clouds, which are then transformed into wireframe models with several million triangles. After reducing the triangles to 20,000–100,000 the 3D models generated in this way can be integrated into virtual 3D environments and then rendered on common AR or VR devices (glasses, tablets) using render engines, such as Unity or Unreal.

A user can then view the virtual 3D persons or objects with VR glasses in the virtual environment from any perspective, which can be used, for example, in a walk-in cinema film (cf. Rommel 2017). This technology can be seen in the video about the pilot production of "Gateway To Infinity" (cf. Fraunhofer Heinrich Hertz Institute 22.04.2017).

Interaction with virtualized persons is not yet possible, but the Heinrich Hertz Institute is working on appropriate technologies and has already demonstrated first promising results.

3.3.4 Summary of Virtual Reality Features

Virtual reality is a computer-generated 3D environment that contains interactive and multisensory elements with which the user interacts in real-time and which he can walk through. The virtual environment completely surrounds him, the real physical world is no longer perceived. All sensory experiences and perceptions are based on computer-generated representations that, through sensory stimuli, convey the feeling of being physically present in the space.

Table 3.1 Identified characteristics of virtual reality

Overview features Virtual reality	
Categories	Features
Application site	Closed virtual environment (indoor/stationary)
Type of use	Mobile and stationary
Room	Walk-in room Three-dimensional synthetic environment Immersive presentation Restricted interaction space Physical presence in space
Contents and media formats	Integration of different media and technologies of multisensory content Audiovisual offers, 360° video, graphics, sound, sensory elements
Interaction and communication	Real-time interaction with space and content Communication with persons is possible
User experience	No perception of the real physical world Presence experience User is in the information Multisensory experience
Technologies	VR system Combination of technologies Recording, input device, sensors, content Closed playback devices (display) Sensor technology
Special feature	Real-time linking with content and users 3D-human body reconstruction (3D-HBR) Integration of people and objects in a virtual environment

Source: own representation

The following overview compiles the features and assigns them to categories. The focus is on content-related and user-specific features (cf. Table 3.1).

3.4 Definition of Mixed Reality

Mixed Reality describes a mixture of virtual parts and the real-physical environment, a mixed reality so to speak. The term was developed in 1994 by Paul Milgram, Haruo Takemura, Akira Utsumi and Funio Kishino for the reality-virtual (RV) continuum (cf. Milgram et al. 1994, p. 282).

3.4.1   Reality-Virtual Continuum

The Reality-Virtual (RV) continuum is a model that categorizes the different gradations of virtual and real representations that, for example, a pilot sees through his semi-transparent HMD (cf. Milgram et al. 1994, p. 284).

Milgram et al. subdivide the different real-physical representations into augmented reality (AR), augmented virtuality (AV) and virtual reality (VR). Mixed reality encompasses the entire spectrum between the real-physical environment and augmented reality with small virtual components. This is contrasted with augmented virtuality (AV) with an almost complete virtual environment (cf. Milgram et al. 1994, p. 283).

The term mixed reality includes augmented reality and augmented virtuality in the spectrum. Unlike augmented reality, mixed reality refers to the mixing or overlaying of real representations and virtual objects (cf. Broll 2013, p. 246).

We speak of mixed reality when the virtual portions predominate. The transitions between a high proportion and too low a proportion of virtual representations are fluid (cf. Dörner et al. 2013, p. 11; Fig. 3.1).

The term Mixed Reality is often used synonymously with Augmented Reality and associated with data glasses such as the HoloLens. Since both cases involve the expansion of the real-physical environment through the integration and overlapping of virtual objects, the terms mixed and augmented reality are used synonymously in this work – in distinction to the above-mentioned product – and summarized under AR. The technical characteristics of mixed reality are similar to those of augmented reality and are briefly described in Sect. 3.5.1.1.

3.4.2   MR Application in the CAVE

The common use for mixed reality is data glasses that integrate virtual objects into the real-physical environment.

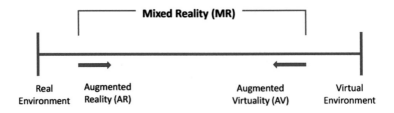

Reality - Virtuality (RV) Continuum

Fig. 3.1 Mixed reality according to Milgram et al., 1994. (Source: own representation)

Fig. 3.2   Illustration of a CAVE engine simulation at Rolls Royce

Another playback option for mixed reality is a CAVE. CAVE stands for Cave Automatic Virtual Environment. This is a multi-sided room, consisting of several projection surfaces, which allows several viewers to view virtual 360° applications (cf. Dörner et al. 2013, p. 20).

The representations on the projection screens create the virtual environment (cf. Craig 2013, p. 22; Fig. 3.2).

In workshop or development scenarios several users can work together on virtual representations via data glasses. They wear semi-transparent data glasses and can recognize the real physical space and the people in it to communicate with them.

3.5   Definition of Augmented Reality

Augmented reality is part of the mixed reality spectrum according to Paul Milgram et al. The term augmented virtuality is no longer used today. Ronald T. Azuma published a comprehensive description of augmented reality in 1997, which he defines as a variation of Virtual Reality. "*Augmented Reality* (AR) is a variation of *Virtual Environments* (VE), or Virtual Reality as it is more commonly called." (Azuma 1997, p. 2, italics in original.)

3.5.1   Features of Augmented Reality

Azuma refers to the definition of Milgram et al. and identifies three characteristics for augmented reality: the combination between virtuality and reality, interaction in real-time and the linking of 3D elements. In distinction to virtual reality, augmented reality involves the real physical world, which means that reality is "visible". Reality or the real-physical world is combined with digital audiovisual media formats such as images, text, videos and sound (cf. Azuma 1997, pp. 2, 9, 10). The integration of 3D objects and 3D people is possible nowadays. The real physical world is thus enriched, supplemented or extended, which corresponds to the English translation of augmented (cf. Messinger et al. 1997, p. 82). In business and science, the English short version AR is used.

The spatial linking of digital information with the real physical world is a special feature of AR. The integrated information is linked with a defined position to the real physical environment, which a user can only see via an augmented reality system (cf. Craig 2013, p. 15 f.). The user receives the information exclusively at the location where the information is located. Unlike VR, all multisensory stimuli are perceived from the real physical environment and are part of the AR experience (cf. Craig 2013, p. 16). Wolfgang Broll describes the characteristics of augmented reality as "an (immediate, interactive and real-time) extension of the perception of the real environment by virtual contents (for any senses), which are oriented as far as possible to reality in their expression and impression, so that in extreme cases (if that is intended) a distinction between real and virtual (sensory) impressions is no longer possible" (Broll 2013, p. 246, the brackets are included in the original). Reality merges with virtuality through artificial or virtual content (cf. Broll 2013, p. 241 f.). This state of perception corresponds to immersion, or the experience of presence as described in the definition of virtual reality (see Sect. 3.3.1).

3.5.1.1 Technical Characteristics and Applications

The AR system is similar to the VR system. It consists of the three technical components sensors, processors and display (cf. Craig 2013, p. 40). AR applications can be used everywhere and mobile via smartphones, tablets and data glasses. The smartphone has the function of the controller and the display. Its position and the viewing angle are tracked by sensors or the satellite geo-positioning system (GPS for short). The environment is recorded with an integrated camera and synchronized with the geo-data, for example, allowing real-time interaction with the content (cf. Broll 2013, pp. 242, 291). As with VR, virtual content is integrated into the real-physical environment. These are graphics, videos, sound, 3D animations, photos, graphs and text (cf. Greiner 2013, p. 319). This content is linked to geodata and only appears at a location defined in the world (cf. Broll 2013, pp. 243, 291). A second way to integrate digital content into space succeeds with special AR Software Development Kits (SDK) like ARCore or ARKit. The digital content is linked to a location in space via an engine such as Unity or Unreal. In order to access the digital content later with the smartphone camera at any location, the respective location of the user is digitally defined. Sensors of an AR-enabled smartphone scan the environment in the process, detecting light differences and movements, which are linked to the digital content in real time (cf. Burke 29.08.2017). The virtual T-Rex in Fig. 3.3 is integrated into the real-physical world via the SDK ARKit/ARCore. The user can photograph such scenes with the smartphone.

Fig. 3.3 Example photo of an AR application

A third possibility is the use of visual markers, in which light-dark effects of the image are used to link them to digital content with the help of the engine. Here too, the digital content is made visible in the real-physical environment via a smartphone camera (cf. Grimm et al. 2013, p. 104 f.). Such image markers can be used, for example, to enhance paintings and objects in a museum or magazines with informative content. The British designer and artist Insa uses them to animate his street art paintings, which can then be viewed via his own AR app (cf. Insa 2019).

Such a "seamless fusion between virtuality and reality" (Broll 2013, p. 291) creates a perfect augmented reality experience.

3.5.2 Summary Augmented Reality

The following table summarizes the AR characteristics.

The real physical world is enriched with digital elements at a specified location, with which the user can interact in real time. The real physical environment and its stimuli are part of the AR experience. In extreme cases, perception between real and virtual sensory impressions is no longer possible (cf. Table 3.2).[3]

---

[3] This description in the table also applies to the definition of mixed reality.

Table 3.2 Overview of features of augmented reality

Categories	Augmented reality
Application site	Real physical environment (inside/outside)
Type of use	Mobile and stationary
Room	Walk-in room Combination of virtual content and real physical world Immersive presentation Large interaction room Physical presence in space
Content and media formats	Integration of different media and technologies of multisensory content Audiovisual offers, 360-degree video, graphics, sound, sensory elements
Interaction and communication	Real-time interaction with space and content Communication with persons is possible
User experience	Perception of the real physical world Presence experience Information comes to the user Multisensory experience Merging the real and virtual world
Technologies	AR system Combination of technologies Recording, input device, sensors Semi-transparent playback devices (display) Radio technology, sensor technology
Special feature	Real-time linking to content and users through GPS CAVE as representation Holoportation Integration of people and objects into a real physical environment

Identified characteristics of augmented reality (source: own representation)

3.6   Comparisons of VR and AR Features

In the previous sections, the terms Virtual, Augmented Mixed Reality were introduced using different definitions. Specific characteristics were identified, categorized and summarized. According to this:

VR is a computer-generated three-dimensional (3D) environment that contains interactive and multisensory elements with which users interact. They can enter the environment in real time. The virtual environment is complete, the real physical world is no longer perceived. All sensory experiences and perceptions are based on the computer-generated representations that, through sensory stimuli, convey the feeling of being physically present in the space.

With AR, the real physical world is enriched with virtual elements at a specified location. The user can interact with these in real time. The real physical environment and its stimuli are part of the AR experience or application. In extreme cases, the perception between real and virtual sensory impressions is no longer possible.

The identified characteristics of VR and AR show similarities, which are analyzed below and combined into a working definition. In this way, commonalities are to be highlighted that enable standardization[4] in order to establish a basis for the media context. The media perspective forms the basis for the analysis of VR and AR as media innovations.

The assignment according to categories has resulted from the characteristics. The focus is on content-related and user-centred characteristics. The differences are highlighted in bold (Table 3.3).

Media-specific properties are found in the categories of space, interaction and communication, and users. These categories form the focus for further analysis in the following. Technical categories are only mentioned in passing but have no significance for the research question in this book.

3.6.1 Categorization of VR and AR Characteristics

AR and VR share common characteristics in the following categories.

Space[5]: Space is a unifying feature in AR and VR. In both media technologies, the space is walkable and integrates the same spatial design principles such as objects, architecture and media formats. The multisensory stimuli influence perception and create immersion. Even though AR and VR spaces differ in the proportion of virtual representations, the fact that a space is designed and manipulated is a common feature of AR and VR. In both cases, the user enters this space and is physically present in it. The difference lies in the gradual representation of the virtual portions.

Content: The integrated formats and media content are the same for VR and AR. The differences lie in the way the content is used. While the information comes to the user in an AR application, the user goes into the information in a VR application.

Interaction and communication: Interaction is possible in AR and VR through body movement, interaction with media content and communication with other people in the room. The differences lie in the type of use.

---

[4]The standardization makes no claim to scientific completeness.

[5]In this work, the concept of space is understood as media space. Following the concept of cyberspace (virtual space), space is understood as a communication space, a physically designed place of action with virtual, social and communicative functions. Aspects of architecture and sociology are integrated (cf. Thiedeke 2014, p. 170). This assumption is supported by the communication scholars Hartmann, Wirth et al. who have developed a hypothesis theory on spatial presence as a reception modality. In it, they make a gradual distinction of the media environment (cf. Hartmann et al. 2005, p. 30).

Table 3.3 Comparison of the identified characteristics of AR and VR

Categories	Augmented reality	Virtual reality
Place of use	Real physical environment (inside/outside)	Closed virtual environment (indoor/stationary)
Type of use	Mobile and stationary	Mobile and stationary
Room	Walk-in room **Combination of virtual content and the real physical world** Immersive presentation **Large interaction room** Physical presence in space	Walk-in room **Three-dimensional synthetic environment** Immersive presentation **Restricted interaction space** Physical presence in space
Contents and Media formats	Integration of different media and technologies multisensory content Audiovisual offers, 360-degree video, graphics, sound, sensory elements	Integration of different media and technologies multisensory content Audiovisual offers, 360-degree video, graphics, sound, sensory elements
Interaction communication	Real-time interaction with space and content Communication with persons is possible	Real-time interaction with space and content Communication with persons is possible
User experience	**Perception of the real physical world** Presence experience **Information comes to the user** Multisensory experience	**No perception of the real physical world** Presence experience **User is in the information** Multisensory experience
Technologies	**AR system** Combination of technologies Recording, input device, sensors, content **Semi-transparent playback devices (display)** Radio technology, sensor technology	**VR system** Combination of technologies Recording, input device, sensors, content **Closed playback devices (display)** Sensor technology
Special feature	Real-time linking to content and users through GPS, markers, etc. **CAVE as a virtual 3D representation** 3D human body reconstruction Holoportation, avatars Virtual integration of persons and objects into the real physical environment	Real-time linking with content and users, makers, etc. **Virtual 3D representations** 3D human body reconstruction Holoportation, avatars Virtual integration of people and objects in a virtual environment

Comparison of the identified characteristics of AR and VR (Source: Own representation)

User experience: With AR and VR, a change in the user's perception of reality occurs, which is conveyed by the media space and the content. The user has the feeling of being physically present in the space. In extreme cases, the medium itself is no longer perceived. The experience of presence is thus a common feature of AR and VR.

The differences between VR and AR experiences lie in the way the media is used. In an AR application, the user designs their media space. Whereas in a VR application, the user enters a designed space that does not exist in the real physical world.

In summary, the **virtual representations of the space,** in gradual differentiation of the virtual parts, the integrated **media content** and the **interaction and communication possibilities** are essential core features of AR and VR. This is complemented by the media effect phenomenon of **immersion**, which gives the user the feeling of being **present in the media space.**

The main difference between AR and VR applications lies in the media experience, i.e. the way in which AR and VR are presented and used. These differences are user-specific and form an important basis for the development of content and possible applications for the media innovations AR and VR (cf. Chap. 5). This difference is not relevant for the following working definition.

3.6.2 Derivation of the Working Definition

Based on the characteristics, the comparison between AR and VR shows that AR and VR have similarities and are comparable to each other. These characteristics could be subsumed under the following working definition:

> Augmented and virtual reality are a) a computer-generated simulation or extension of a real-physical environment as a **three-dimensional media space** (space), which b) contains computer-based **virtual 2D and 3D representations** (content), in which c) the user can **interact and communicate in** an interactive, virtual or augmented reality by means of **his physical presence and activity** (body) in d) real time (interaction) and e) experiences a multisensory extension of **reality perception** (user experience).[6]

The characteristics of space, content, interaction and communication as well as the user experience can be summarized in the **two categories of content** and **user.** The content category considers the media space, the content offerings and the interaction and communication with these, while the user category considers the user experience with an AR and VR application (Table 3.4).

The two categories of content and user thus form the basis for the expert interviews. These are analyzed in Chap. 7 in order to find success factors for the development of content and AR and VR applications from the producer perspective.

---

[6] This working definition is derived from the features identified in this chapter and has been expanded to include characteristic features. The definition is verified on the basis of the expert interviews in Chap. 7.

Table 3.4 Brief overview of the categories from this chapter

Categories	Subcategories
Content	Media space, content, interaction and communication
Users	User experience of media use, interaction, space, body

Source: Own representation

3.7   Conclusion

This chapter has set the stage to identify the characteristic features of AR and VR. It introduces the concepts through possible applications. The aim is to understand AR and VR as media in order to bring content and user-related aspects to the fore for this research. That AR and VR are media has been made clear by the excursus on media history. According to this, the creation of virtual spaces and illusion spaces is part of media history, which AR and VR stringently continue. Based on the characteristics of AR and VR, a working definition was developed and the categories of content and user were formed.

They represent the first basis for the analysis of the success factors.

Literature

AWE Augmented Wold Expo (2019); URL: https://www.awexr.com/about_awe, Abruf am 16.10.2019.

Azuma, Ronald T. (1997): A Survey of Augmented Reality, in: Presence: Teleoperators and Virtual Environments, 6, Nr. 4, S. 355–385. URL: http://www.cs.unc.edu/~azuma/ARpresence.pdf, Abruf am 30.10.2019.

Broll, Wolfgang (2013): Augmentierte Realität, in: Dörner, Ralf; Broll, Wolfgang; Grimm, Paul; Jung, Berhanrd (Hrsg.): Virtual und Augmented Reality (VR/AR), Heidelberg: Springer-Verlag, S. 241–294.

Burke, Dave (29. August 2017): ARCore: Augmented reality at Android scale URL: https://android--developers.googleblog.com/2017/08/arcore-augmented-reality-at-android.html,   Abruf   am 30.10.2019.

Craig, Alan B. (2013): Understanding Augmented Reality – Concepts and Applications, Waltham: Morgan Kaufmann.

Deuerling, Tanja (2015): Innovationsmanagement für neues Fernsehen – Entwicklungen von Bewegtbildformaten in Abhängigkeit vom Innovationsgrad, Wiesbaden: Springer VS.

Dörner, Ralf et al. (2013): Einleitung, in: Dörner, Ralf; Broll, Wolfgang; Grimm, Pau; Jung, Bernhard (Hrsg.): Virtual und Augmented Reality (VR/AR), Heidelberg: Springer-Verlag, S. 1–31.

Fraunhofer Heinrich Hertz Institut (22.04.2017): Making of – Gateway to Infinity, YouTube, URL: https://www.youtube.com/watch?v=8h6i2_3xDcs, Abruf am 30.10.2019.

Fröhlich, Kerstin (2008): Organisation für Innovation, Kreativfördernde Oragnisation in der TV-Unterhaltungsproduktion, in: G. Siegert; B. von Rimscha (Hrsg.): Zur Ökonomie der UNterhaltungsproduktion. Köln, S. 151–173.

Grau, Oliver (2001): Telepräsenz. Zu Genealogie und Epistemologie von Interaktion und Simulation, in: Peter Gendolla (Hrsg.): Formen interaktiver Medienkunst: Geschichte, Tendenzen, Utopien, Suhrkamp: Frankfurt am Main, S. 39–63, URL: http://sammelpunkt.philo.at/579/1/Grau2.pdf, Abruf am 30.10.2019.

Greiner, Matthias, (2013): Augmentierte Realität und Print, in: Dörner, Ralf; Broll, Wolfgang; Grimm, Paul; Jung, Bernhard (Hrsg.): Virtual und Augmented Reality (VR/AR), Heidelberg: Springer-Verlag, S. 318–319.

Grimm, Paul, Rigo, Herold, Hummel, Johannes, Broll, Wolfgang (2013): VR-Eingabegeräte, in: Dörner, Ralf; Broll, Wolfgang; Grimm, Paul; Jung, Bernhard (Hrsg.): Virtual und Augmented Reality (VR/AR), Heidelberg: Springer-Verlag, S. 97–125.

Hartmann, Tilo; Böcking, Saskia Schramm, Holger; Wirth, Werner; Klimmt, Christoph; Vorderer, Peter (2005): Räumliche Präsenz als Rezeptionsmodalität. Ein theoretisches Modell zur Entstehung von Präsenzerleben, URL: https://www.researchgate.net/publication/257158657_Raumliche_Prasenz_als_Rezeptionsmodalitat_Ein_theoretisches_Modell_zur_Entstehung_von_Prasenzerleben, Abruf am 30.10.2019.

Hickethier, Knut (2012): Film und Fernsehanalyse, 5. Aufl., Stuttgart: J.B. Metzler Verlag.

IEEE Library (30.10.2019a) Suchbegriff: Virtual Reality, URL: https://www.ieee.org/searchresults/index.html?q=virtual+reality#gsc.tab=0&gsc.q=virtual%20reality&gsc.page=1, Abruf am 30.10.2019.

IEEE Library (30.12.2019b) Suchbegriff: Augmented Reality, URL: https://www.ieee.org/searchresults/index.html?q=Augmented+Reality#gsc.tab=0&gsc.q=Augmented%20Reality&gsc.page=1, Abruf am 30.10.2019.

Insa (2019): Gifi-iti, URL: https://gif-iti.tumblr.com/ Abruf am 30.10.2019.

Janssen, Jan-Keno (2018): Raumbild – Ein Besuch in Microsofts Aufnahmestudio für volumetrisches Video, in CT Ausgabe 13/2018, Hannover, Heise Medien GmbH & Co. KG, URL: https://www.heise.de/select/ct/2018/13/1529634800384566, Abruf am 16.10.2019.

Kayyali, M. Saleh (30.05.2012): Ivan Sutherland: Sketchpad Demo, YouTube, URL: https://www.youtube.com/watch?v=6orsmFndx_o, Abruf 30.10.2019.

Lanier, Jaron (2018): Aufbruch in eine neue Zeit, Hamburg, Hoffmann und Campe Verlag.

Laval Virtual (2019): URL: https://www.laval-virtual.com/ Abruf am 16.10.2019.

Mann, Steve; Havens, John C.; et al. (08.04.2018): All Reality – Values, taxonomy, and continuum, for Virtual, Augmented, eXtended/MiXed (X), Mediated (X,Y), and Multimediated Reality/Intelligence, Conell University, URL: https://arxiv.org/pdf/1804.08386.pdf, Abruf am 30.10.2019.

Messinger, Heinz et al. (1997): Langenscheidts Großes Schulwörterbuch Englisch-Deutsch, 13. Aufl., Berlin: Langenscheidt.

Milgram, Paul; Takemura, Haruo, Utsumi, Akira, Kishino, Fumio (1994): Augmented Reality: A class of displays on the reality-virtuality, SPIE Vol. 2351, Telemanipulator and Telepresence Technologies, S. 282–292, URL: http://etclab.mie.utoronto.ca/publication/1994/Milgram_Takemura_SPIE1994.pdf, Abruf am 30.10.2019.

Microsoft (2019): Mixed reality Capture Studios, URL: https://www.microsoft.com/en-us/mixed-reality/capture-studios, Abruf 30.10.2019.

Mühlberger, Andreas (2014): Virtuelle Realität in der Klinischen Emotions- und Psychotherapieforschung, in: Jeschke, Sabine; Kobbelt, Leif; Dröge, Alicia (Hrsg.): Exploring Virtuality, Wiesbaden: Springer Fachmedien, S. 149–161.

Rommel, Anna (2017): Die neue Dimension der Immersion: 3D-Human Body Reconstruction, Fraunhofer Heinrich Hertz Institut, URL: https://www.hhi.fraunhofer.de/das-fraunhofer-hhi/ueber-uns/geschichte-des-hhi/90-jahre-hhi/die-neue-dimension-der-immersion-3d-human-body-reconstruction.html, Abruf 30.10.2019.

Sadowski, W.; Stanney, K.M. (2002): Presence in virtual environments, in: Stanney, K.M. (Hrsg.). Handbook of virtual environments: Design, implementation and applications, Mahwah: IEA, S. 791–806, URL: http://w3.uqo.ca/cyberpsy/index.php/immersion-presence/, Abruf am 30.10.2019.

Scholze-Stubenrecht, Werner et al. (2006): Duden: Die deutsche Rechtschreibung, 24. Aufl., Bd. 1, Mannheim: Dudenverlag, Bibliographisches Institut & F.A. Brockhaus.

Schreer, Oliver; Feldmann, Ingo; Kauff, Peter et al. (17.10.2019): Lessons Learnt during One Year of Commercial Volumetric Video Production, Proceedings of IBC conference, Amsterdam, Netherlands, September 2019, URL: https://www.ibc.org/create-and-produce/lessons-learnt-during-one-year-of-commercial-volumetric-video-production/5087.article, Download: https://www.ibc.org/download?ac=10506, Abruf am 30.10.2017.

Stoppe, Sebastian (2016): "Getting Immersed in Star Trek, Storytelling Between "True" and "False" on the Holodeck", in SFRA Review (316): S. 4–15. URL: https://sfra.wildapricot.org/resources/Documents/SFRA%20316.pdf, Abruf am 30.10.2019.

Sutherland, Ivan (1965): The Ultimate Display Ivan E. Sutherland Information Processing Techniques Office, ARPA, OSD Proceedings of IFIP Congress, S. 506–508, URL: http://worrydream.com/refs/Sutherland%20-%20The%20Ultimate%20Display.pdf, Abruf am 30.10.2019.

Thiedeke, Udo (2014): Weiße Elefanten für alle! Sinnhorizont und Normalitätserwartungen bei interaktionsmedialer Kommunikation, in: Jeschke, Sabine; Kobbelt, Leif; Dröge; Alicia (Hrsg.): Exploring Virtuality, Wiesbaden: Springer Fachmedien, S. 162–172.

VR Days Europe (2019); URL: https://vrdays.co/, Abruf am 30.10.2019.

AR and VR in the Media Context

4

> *From the point of view of media science, immersive media develop the concept of media further.*

The following chapter defines AR and VR as media and identifies the media-specific characteristics using the concept of media. This is based on the assumption that VR and AR are new media as the characteristics of space, content, interaction and user experience identified in Chap. 3 correspond to media-specific characteristics. The media context focuses on content, economic and user-related aspects of AR and VR, which are relevant for identifying success factors for content production. The aim is to use these success factors to derive principles that will help develop concepts for content production. It is known from media history that "media […] develop their own forms of impact. One can also say that they have their own ›curriculum‹ which each user has to operate in order to experience something through the respective medium. […] each mediality imposes different requirements on the human body." (Schmidt 2000, p. 188; Faßler and Halbach 1998, p. 33). Schmidt refers to the close connection between medium, identity and culture and the processes of change that new media cause (cf. Schmidt 2000, p. 188). To illustrate this dimension of the necessary change processes, Section 4.1 presents the vision of Virtual and Augmented Reality. In Sect. 4.2 the concept of media is introduced from the perspective of media and communication studies and applied to AR and VR in Sect. 4.2.3. It becomes clear that AR and VR are immersive media and that their specific characteristics make them media innovations: This aspect is elaborated in Sect. 4.3. Section 4.4 deals with the acceptance of media innovations. The innovation reference is the basis for determining media innovations.

© The Author(s), under exclusive license to Springer-Verlag GmbH, DE, part of Springer Nature 2023
E. Langer, *Media Innovations AR and VR*,
https://doi.org/10.1007/978-3-662-66280-9_4

4.1   The Media Visions of AR and VR

The following excursus illustrates the medial and communicative potential attributed to AR and VR by its developers and that the concept of media for augmented and virtual reality can be expanded to include new dimensions. Jaron Lanier described in the early 1990s said dimensions. According to the virtual reality pioneer, VR is a medium that will make possible a new form of communication. A form of communication in which people instead of using words create worlds and dreams they can share with each other. Lanier envisions a spontaneous and expressive conversation without symbols. "[...] a new kind of communication. It's really putting people inside your dreams, and something that's very hard to describe, because it's a mode of communication; I think that's really different than description. [...] You might call it the collective conscious." (Lanier 1989, pp. 7–18, quoted from Ommeln 2008, p. 106) Lanier sees VR as a medium of communication and equates the virtual world with the real physical world, but without its physical limits yet with room for fantasy. "[...] turn this building into a tulip [...] in the virtual world you can. [This] gives us this sense of being able to be who we are without limitation; for our imagination to become objective and shared with other people." (Lanier 1989, pp. 7–18, cited in Slater and Sanchez-Vives 2016, p. 2) Physical and spatial properties are dissolved in virtual reality and have their own laws. Such imaginings open up endless possibilities for media content of all kinds. This raises questions about new rules and ethical consequences, which the philosophers Thomas Metzinger and Michael Madary, for example, address in their publication "Real Virtuality: A Code of Ethical Conduct." In it, they explicitly advocate ethical rules and point out that the way humans perceive their natural environment must be taken into account, especially in VR, since VR creates new environments that are experienced more intensively. Metzinger and Madary assume that VR will not only change the general image of humanity, but also our understanding of deeply rooted notions of self-perception, authenticity or reality. They expect structural changes in the world that will produce novel forms of everyday social interactions and change the kind of social relationships people have known so far[1] (cf. Metzinger and Madary 19.02.2016, p. 2 f.). These examples show that a media and communication science approach is useful to understand AR and VR in their media complexity. Both sciences offer different focal points for this purpose. Media studies deals with media content, reception and media economics. Communication studies looks at the forms of communication of media, their impact and their economic and social influence (cf. Uhrig 2015, p. 14).

---

[1] Metzinger and Madary refer to their EU project "Virtual Embodiment and Robot Re-Embodiment" (VERE). The focus was on researching self-perception and illusions of self-embodiment, according to which the user has the feeling of owning and controlling a body that is not his own, but like an avatar in VR (cf. VERE 2010).

4.2   Definition of Media

In the following, Augmented Reality (AR) and Virtual Reality (VR) are defined as media. For this purpose the characteristic features of new media or digital media are introduced and applied to AR and VR.

4.2.1   Media Theoretical Context

The concept of media is based on a variety of theories and models. The media scientist Werner Faulstich points out that "a comprehensive scientifically [accepted] theory of "the" medium [...] does not yet exist". (Faulstich 2004, p. 18) This is because there is no comprehensive media history yet. In order to understand the theoretical structure of this thesis, the theories and models of thought relevant to the media reference of AR and VR will be presented. Media studies refer to a film, book or piece of music as a medium. This is based on individual theories for theatre, film and television, which examine the medium in terms of its content-related statement and formal aesthetics with regard to its reception by the recipient (cf. Faulstich 2004, pp. 14, 16). Communication studies consider media in the context of social communication processes as the means of transmitting information as communication (cf. Dogruel 2013, p. 260; Böhn and Seidler 2008, p. 20). Several communication and media theories exist for this purpose, such as mass media theory and systems theory media theory (cf. Faulstich 2004, p. 14). The concept of media in these theories depends on their research focus.

In the theory of mass media, the communicative and social modes of functioning of a dissemination medium are at the centre of research. In the systems theory approach, the medium is ascribed an overarching cultural and social significance. For example, money is a medium of interaction or exchange with social functions (cf. Faulstich 2004, p. 16). The constructivist approach in media research considers the interaction of media and their perception by the recipient. In this thesis, the constructivist approach[2] is primarily considered, as it allows for a broad concept of media.

The constructivist approach includes the human being as a psychological system in the consideration of media and media effects: Human beings are part of the communication process, their ideas and perceptions, according to the literary and media scientist Matthias Mertens, have an influence on the construction of reality. These ideas and perceptions in turn have an effect on the media effect. Mertens extends the constructivist approach by

---

[2]Constructivism is not a uniform theory but pursues different approaches in different disciplines. Schmidt draws on sociological, biological-neuroscientific, cybernetic and philosophical as well as psychological aspects. The term construction is used to represent a process that generates constructions of reality depending on biological, sociocultural and cognitive conditions. According to Schmidt, reality is only created through observation and the way in which observation is made. This leads to actions and thus to communication (cf. Schmidt 1994, pp. 4, 5).

seeing media as reality producers that influence reality through economic striving and efficiency (cf. Schmidt 2000, pp. 76, 80, 82 f.). In relation to AR and VR, the constructivist approach is relevant in three ways. The constructivist approach places the user at the centre, who, according to the characteristics in Chap. 3, is himself a medium within the medium. The broad concept of media enables the integration of the virtuality of space as a place of communication and media and deals with the concept of reality generated by the media, which is on the user-related as well as on the economic side.

In connection with constructivist theory, the concept of media by the Canadian media theorist Marshall McLuhan is used, who offers a comprehensive definition of media. McLuhan refers to all existing objects and signs as media that can be perceived through the human senses. He includes speech, facial expressions and all real and virtual objects. What is communicated is irrelevant, since according to him the medium itself does the communicating: "The medium is the message." (McLuhan 1964, p. 1 f.). McLuhan understands media as extensions of the human body and human senses, which he calls "Extentions of Man" (cf. McLuhan 1964 p. 2 f.; Beck 2003, p. 73 f.). In McLuhan's sense media are tools shaped by humans, which in turn shape humans (Hemmerling 2014, p. 113). As a medium, media change the perception and perspectives of communicative and cultural structures. As a consequence, social processes appear in a new perspective, which gives room to new courses of action. This in turn influences the media in interaction (cf. Schmidt 2000, p. 80; Dogruel 2013, p. 89). A line of thought that primarily refers to communicative processes.

4.2.2   Derivation of the Concept of Media

The concept of media still valid today follows the definition of Ulrich Saxer, who divides media into four specific characteristics: (1) technical communication channels, (2) sign systems (3) organizations and (4) constitutional institutions (cf. Faulstich 2004, p. 18; Dogruel 2013, p. 263). According to this, media have a **1st communication channel** that ensures the distribution of content. The **2nd sign systems** are symbols, icons such as letters, pictures, moving images (videos), graphics, which convey meaning and, through the codes and signs used, prescribe a constituted formal and content-related mode of reception as a process of understanding. They enable interaction and communication, understood as intentional communicative exchange in a process of understanding. Symbols and signs are based on socially understood norms that are situated in a social context. **3rd Organizations** are the structures and actors within a media system that perform services in a specific function according to media economic principles. These are media companies, publishers, production companies and agencies and their actors. **4th Institutions** provide "sets of rules" such as modes of production, use and presentation. They are meant to give the actors structural orientation and help to assign meaning to their projects. In doing so, they permanently define roles, norms and modes of communication (cf. Saxer 1999, cited in Droguel 2013, pp. 15, 80; Beck 2003, p. 74 f.).

New media are the further development of previous media based on a new media technology that has a communicative function (cf. Garncarz 2009, p. 65; Dogruel 2013, p. 24). The term new media is used synonymously with digital media, which refers to the specific feature of computer-based production of content and the fact that it is consumed on computer (cf. Dogruel 2013, p. 65; Beck 2003, pp. 72, 76). In this paper, the term digital media is used. Digital media complement Saxer's media characteristics with specific criteria. For better understanding, they are numbered consecutively.

Characteristic features of digital media are: **5th the combination of media formats** and their **integration into other media** (cf. Beck 2003, p. 77; Dogruel 2013, p. 80). Media formats such as text, graphics, images and video are combined through computer processing and new media content is created from them, such as video games, video series, infographics, blogs, which in turn are integrated into media, such as an internet platform, for dissemination purposes. Media content follows content-related and formal design principles, which are subdivided according to genre and category[3] and presented in a specific way for a defined purpose of use via selected channels for communication purposes to a specific group of users (cf. Dogruel 2013, p. 262; Beck 2003, p. 77 f.). Media integration is only made possible by digitization, which leads to media convergence. 6. **Media convergence** is a characteristic of digital media and describes the convergence and growing together of media and different media content. It leads to changes on the provider and supply side and, from a media economics perspective, influences the value chain of the players in the media system (cf. Löffelholz and Thorsten 2003, p. 29; Beck 2003, pp. 79, 85). **7. Interactivity and media networking** are specific characteristics of new media (cf. Dogruel 2013, p. 80; Beck 2003, p. 81). Through them, new communication offers can be provided, e.g. chats and blogs, which change communication processes. Thereby, the roles of sender, producer and consumer can change (cf. Beck 2003, pp. 76, 83, 84). Interactivity opens up the return channel for the user, who becomes a producer and can create and distribute his or her own media products. **8** Digital media are characterized by **spatial and temporal unrestricted use** (cf. Dogruel 2013, p. 80; Wolling and Kuhlmann 2003, p. 132 f.). The immediate transmission of media content in real time influences the user's perception of reality, which thereby creates a reality of its own. This is based on the communication science theory of constructivism, according to which media influence reality, which is first established by them (cf. Hickethier 2012, p. 10).

The examination of medial realities is discussed in digital media with computer games. In this context, the "virtual reality, simulation of reality [...] and the dissolution between reality and fiction" (Faulstich 2004, p. 31) is mentioned, which Faulstich calls

---

[3] Genres are narrative forms and themes that are similar in structure and content, such as love stories or thrillers. Genre are cross-media terms and are also found in literature and theatre. Hickethier attributes to genre a stimulating and affect-controlling function for the user. In distinction to genre, categories are aesthetic aspects that offer orientation for the user and create expectations through their structure (cf. Hickethier 2012, p. 208).

hypermedial and which unfolds its sense-expanding capabilities in VR video games (cf. Beck 2003, p. 78).

9 Virtuality is thus a specific feature of digital media (cf. Dogruel 2013, p. 80, Klimmt et al. 2005, p. 422 f.), as generated by computer games and VR. The term virtuality indicates the artificiality of media such as computer games, referring to their digital, intangible form. In the context, the term immersion is used. According to this, digital media stimulate the user in such a way that the user no longer perceives the real physical environment and merges with the medium. The media-mediated state referred to as immersion is created by the power of the medium, which draws the user's complete attention to itself (cf. Sect. 3.3.1; Rittmann 2008, p. 47; Witmer and Singer 1998, p. 227; Hofer 2013, p. 281). The term immersive media is used for media that create a high level of immersion. The phenomenon of immersion is well known in media and cultural studies in the reception and effects of images, film and other media (cf. Section 3.1; Uhrig 2015, p. 78; Grau 2001, p. 39 f.).

4.2.3   Definition of Immersive Media AR and VR

The media-specific characteristics of digital media defined above will be applied to AR and VR in the following to refer to them as media and immersive media, respectively. AR and VR are thus immersive media with the following media characteristics:

1. AR and VR systems whose communication channels are smartphones and data glasses.
2. The sign systems of AR and VR are the 2D and 3D representations that combine more signs to create new media content.
3. The organizational structure for an AR and VR media system is currently emerging at different levels, with actors and organizations creating ecosystems that are not inherent in the media system (see Sect. 6.1).
4. There are not yet any institutionalizations that lay down universally applicable rules and norms. Since these are new types of media, new forms, norms and approaches to rules and regulations are being developed (cf. Section 4.2.2).
5. The combination and integration of media formats and content is a key feature of AR and VR.
6. This continues the media convergence.
7. The possibility to interact with content is a characteristic feature of AR and VR.
8. Spatiotemporally independent use is not possible because the content is spatially associated with a specific location, which is a characteristic feature of VR and AR.
9. Immersion and the experience of presence and the associated perception of the user are specific characteristics of AR and VR.

This list shows that Saxer's concept of media and the characteristics of digital media can be applied to AR and VR (cf. Section 4.2.2). However, there are three differences to digital media: (1) the **spatio-temporally linked use,** (2) the **three-dimensionality of space and the user,** who (3) is **present in the medium.** The starting point is the working definition, according to which AR and VR are

> a) a computer-generated simulation or extension of a real-physical environment as a **three-dimensional media space** (space), in which c) the user can interact and communicate b) through computer-supported virtual 2D and 3D representations (content), in an interactive, virtual or augmented reality by means of **his physical presence and activity** (body) in d) real time (interaction) and e) experiences a **multi-sensory** extension of the perception of reality (user experience) (cf. Section 3.6.1 f.).

For AR and VR, the spatial dimension and the linking of the content and the physicality of the user with the space are of central importance. These features do not appear in previous media definitions.

Accordingly, the immersive media AR and VR have the following characteristics: The characteristics of Digital Media 1–9 are adopted and extended by the media-specific characteristic of the three-dimensionality of space and user. Feature 8, which describes the spatio-temporally independent user, is replaced by the specific feature of the spatio-temporal linking of content and user with space.

Based on the media-specific characteristics, factors were identified that expand the categories from Sect. 3.6.2. Accordingly, three-dimensionality and the link between space, content and user are to be integrated in the categories content and user. The categories contain media-specific characteristics. They form the basis for the expert interviews, which are intended to provide indications of success factors for implementation criteria in the respective categories. An overview of the categories identified is presented in Sect. 4.5.

4.3   Media Innovations AR and VR

The task of this publication is to identify success factors that are relevant for content production for AR and VR. The research question investigates which content- and production-related factors are necessary to successfully produce applications for the immersive media AR and VR. The investigation is conducted from the perspective of the producers.

The following section describes AR and VR as media innovations. The innovation context focuses on economic and production-related factors, as it is assumed that economic and structural conditions influence the development of novel products. The innovation context will be used to identify further categories that indicate success factors.

4.3.1   Definition of Media Innovation

The term media innovation is a word combination of the terms media and innovation. The term media was described in the previous chapter and applied to VR and AR. The term innovation is derived from the Latin verb innovare, which is translated as to renew. The noun innovatio means innovation, renewal or change (cf. Georges 1918; Scholze-Stubenrecht et al. 2006, p. 533). In summary, media innovations are renewals or novelties in the media context. On the economic level, innovations are divided into the dimensions of product, process, management and their impact on the value chain (cf. Dogruel 2013, pp. 250, 252). In this context, business models can themselves be innovations (cf. Stähler 2001, p. 36 f.). In media and communication studies, innovations are described as external influencing factors "that lead to changes in, for example, value creation processes and business models" (Dogruel 2013, p. 52; Kiefer 2005, p. 161; Küng 2008, p. 4 f.). For companies, innovations are an economic driving force to compete in markets (Fröhlich 2010, p. 94, Behrends 2001, p. 17). In the context of communication studies, media innovations are novel products, services and management processes whose impact on the value chain of the actors leads to change processes at the economic and societal level (cf. Dogruel 2013, p. 298).

According to Dogruel, two aspects are at the forefront of determining media innovations. They lead to changes in communication processes and have an impact on economic structures, for example when new actors enter the market and produce new products (cf. Dogruel 2013, p. 299 f.). "Only when new media show effects on (interpersonal, group, public) communication processes and structures can they be characterized as media innovations." (Dogruel 2013, p. 304) Here it must be mentioned that the innovation reference is to mass media. Even if AR and VR do not (yet) have a mass media function, the term media innovation still applies to them, as companies worldwide are striving to develop them into mass media (cf. Sects. 1.1 and 6.1.1).

In research on media economics, media content is referred to as innovation because the production of innovative and up-to-date media content is demanded by clients and audiences and this is the occasion for a constant process of creating new types of media content (cf. Fröhlich 2010, p. 21 f.; Vahs and Buhrmester 2002, p. 9; Kiefer 2001, p. 178). Thus, the development and production of innovations in the form of media content are an essential part of the media industry. Research in media economics is oriented towards economics and its concept of innovation (cf. Fröhlich 2010, p. 35).

4.3.2   Economic Concept of Innovation

The concept of innovation in economics is based on a number of concepts, two of which are examined in more detail here and applied to AR and VR. According to Joseph Schumpeter, innovations are creative destruction through the recombination of means of production and their economic exploitation possibilities (cf. Schumpeter 1912, p. 159). Schumpeter describes the innovation process as a stepwise linear process, which he divides into a three-phase model: the development of the idea or invention (1. Invention), which is further developed by the company into novel, marketable products (2. Innovation) and, by meeting user needs, is established in the market (3. Diffusion) (Dogruel 2013, pp. 143,

171; Schumpeter (1961) p. 110). Hauschildt and Salomo focus on the novelty of an innovation that is ""noticeably" different from the comparable and has a useful purpose" (cf. Hauschildt and Salomo 2011, pp. 4, 6, in the original text the word noticeably is highlighted by quotation marks). For Hauschildt and Salomo, the useful aspect is analogous to Schumpeter's user need, according to which the establishment of an innovation in the market presupposes the fulfilment of user needs.

The economic sciences characterize innovations as radical and incremental, or revolutionary and evolutionary innovations (cf. Hauschildt and Salomo 2011, p. 13). This allows a statement about novelty on different levels. Radical innovations "occur at early stages of a product's life cycle" (Stähler, Patrick, 2001, p. 71), create new markets and industries, and are accompanied by large productivity surges developed by companies outside the industry. The effects of radical or revolutionary innovations entail changes in important areas in the company and in the market (cf. Hauschildt and Salomo 2011, p. 16).

With regard to AR and VR, the following aspects can be derived from the concept of innovation in economics. According to Schumpeter's model, the invention phase, which defines the invention of technology and products, has been completed with regard to AR and VR. The innovation has been developed into products in the form of applications. In this respect, AR and VR can be described as innovation in Schumpeter's processual sense. Marketable products that meet a user need are currently being worked on in all sectors (cf. Sections 1.1 and 6.1.1). According to Schumpeter, this corresponds to phase 3 of the innovation process.

For Schumpeter, as for Hauschildt and Salomo, the benefit aspect is a central factor for the establishment of an innovation in the market. Accordingly, the solution of a user need determines whether and how the media innovations AR and VR will establish themselves profitably. Radical innovations for AR and VR applications can be seen in the fact that work is being done on walk-infilms and immersive media are establishing themselves in sectors that previously did not produce any media products (cf. Sections 3.3.2 and 6.1). Production thrusts can be observed above all on the side of the equipment manufacturers (cf. Sect. 1.1).

It is characteristic of media innovations that an economic evaluation of media innovations through digitization processes only takes place when specific applications become established among users and viable business and revenue models develop from this (cf. Dogruel 2013, p. 304). According to Dogruel, the exploitability of media innovations should therefore be understood as a process on several levels, which takes place through social and economic interactions, as well as a heterogeneous composition of actors, and can therefore be planned to a limited extent. In particular the process on the user side, which is based on social attribution of meaning and the formation of user contexts and practices, makes it difficult to steer for acceptance and implementation in the market (cf. Dogruel 2010, pp. 204, 318, 320). This implies that users and their needs must be central in the further innovation process in order to build market interest for media innovations. This is because only demand on the user side and the associated differentiation of media offerings creates a demand market (cf. Schmidt 2000, p. 190).

4.3.3 Summary

The positioning of AR and VR as media innovations shows that fulfilling a user need is a central task for successfully establishing the immersive media AR and VR in the market. As the market for VR and AR is currently emerging and different players are involved who were previously little or not at all familiar with the production of media productions, it can be assumed that market-changing trends will develop which will exert an influence on the value chain of media producers (cf. Sects. 1.1 and 6.1.1). On the other hand, the processes of change also offer the potential for new types of business models that develop through user needs based on specific characteristics of AR and VR. The identification of user needs therefore forms a central task for the innovation development process. To design such processes, Hauschildt and Salomo offer methods for processes in the company (micro level) and for market strategy (macro level), among others, by asking questions such as: What is new for whom and how? (cf. Hauschildt and Salomo 2011, p. 18).

A detailed presentation of these or other methods would go beyond the scope of this paper.[4] Approaches to this are presented in Sect. 5.2.1.

Knowledge of methods is requested during the expert interviews, as it is assumed that knowledge of methods favours the development of products for AR and VR that meet a user need.

4.4 Acceptance of Media Innovations

According to the theory of Schumpeter and Hauschildt et al. AR and VR are in phase 3 of the innovation process. The benefits of AR and VR do not yet seem to have arrived at the market level. Offerings that fulfill a user need are missing. This hypothesis is confirmed by the low willingness to engage with the immersive media AR and VR (cf. Sect. 1.1). The reasons for this are attributed to high acquisition costs for VR devices (cf. Steger, Johannes 10.07.2017). In order for media to be used, they need a natural application that contributes to coping with everyday routines, entertainment and the satisfaction of individual needs (cf. Bonfadelli et al. 2010, p. 621).

According to the diffusion theory of sociologist Everett M. Rogers, a lack of knowledge or incorrect knowledge leads to uncertainty on the part of the user and makes it more difficult for the user to accept innovations (cf. Rogers 2003, p. 13). Diffusion theory understands the acceptance and adoption (adaptation) of innovations as a five-stage communication process in which the decision in favour of an innovation at the user level depends essentially on knowledge about it, the type of user and his willingness to engage

---

[4] Methods for innovation development at the market level would be e.g. Business Model Innovation, at the product development level e.g. Design Thinking. Both methods take into account user and market perspectives for the development of innovations (cf. Grots and Pratschke 2009, p. 18 f.; Brown 2008, p. 84 f.; Stähler 2001, p. 36, 77).

with the innovation, and his social environment (Rogers 2003, pp. 20 f., 172 f.). At the product level Rogers sees five quality characteristics that favor a decision in favor of an innovation: (1) Relative advantage on an economic or social level, e.g. through simpler, more favorable handling, the fulfillment of desires and needs and the enhancement of social standing, (2) the possibility of integration (compatibility) into the system of values and norms of a user or a group, (3) ease of use (complexity), (4) the possibility of trying out an innovation (trialability) in order to interest potential users, for example through easy availability or free use as well as lighthouse projects, and (5) the generation of experience through observation (observability) in the narrower social circle. The easier it is for a user to observe the insights of other users, the more willing they are to try out the innovation (cf. Rogers 2003, p. 15 f., 221 f.; Karnowski 2013, p. 514).

According to Rogers, the adaptation process depends on different types of users. Depending on each other, a small number of innovators adopt the innovation at an early stage (2.5%). These are followed by early adopters. These are often opinion leaders and play an important role in the diffusion process (13.5%). A subsequent early majority (Early Majority) opens the way to the mass market, the late majority (Late Majority) and laggards adapt innovations only after they are established (cf. Karnowski 2013, p. 519 f.; Rogers 2003, p. 22). The diffusion theory is methodologically criticized because the diffusion process is understood as a linear one that does not take into account influences from actors, for example from social media. In this context, the theory has not been further developed (cf. Karnowski 2013, p. 523). The diffusion theory is relevant for this work in that it enables a classification in terms of market establishment and user acceptance for the media innovations AR and VR.

4.4.1 Acceptance of AR and VR

The following aspects can be derived from this for the adaptation and acceptance of AR and VR media: The user and his needs are important criteria for a successful integration of the media into everyday life. Taking into account the four key factors according to Roger's diffusion theory, communicative measures such as knowledge and experience reports could develop social acceptance on the one hand. The qualitative criteria would be possible through offerings that integrate into daily media use and provide a subjective user value that other media do not enable. On the other hand AR and VR do not have the media value with the user as mass media (compatibility). An AR app would currently be just another app on the smartphone whose usefulness has yet to be proven to the user. In addition media innovations only become established when they have a viable business model (cf. Sects. 4.3.2 and 4.4). These indications support the assumption that the satisfaction of user needs can increase acceptance of VR and AR and that indications of success factors for the media innovations AR and VR can be found here.

Table 4.1 Overview of the categories for media consideration

Categories	Subcategories
1. Content	Media format, story, three-dimensionality space and content, Interaction and communication, linking space and content
2. Users	User experience of media usage, Interaction and communication experience
3. Economy	Production and production method Economic and structural framework conditions

Overview of the categories from this chapter (Own representation)

4.5   Conclusion

In this chapter, AR and VR were defined as immersive media. The specific media characteristics of the three-dimensionality of space, the physically present user in three-dimensional space, and the user experience were elaborated. In addition the linking of space and information was identified as a media-specific characteristic. These characteristics were added to the categories of content and user.

The novelty of the immersive media AR and VR was examined using the concept of innovation. According to Schumpeter, Hauschildt and Salomo's understanding of innovation, innovation is a process that results in changes at the market and company level. On the product level, the prerequisite for a successful establishment of AR and VR is the fulfillment of user needs. Accordingly, on the economic side, the fulfillment of user needs represents a success factor. According to the diffusion theory, the market establishment of media innovations depends on user acceptance, which can only occur when users recognize the advantages of immersive media and have easy access to the media.

The research question about the success factors for the production of content for AR and VR therefore examines on the one hand novel products that fulfill a user need and on the other hand the framework conditions necessary for this.

For this purpose the third category **economy** is added. The three categories **content**, **user** and **economy** form the main categories (see Table 4.1).

Literature

Beck, Klaus (2003): Neue Medien – neue Theorie? in: Löffelholz, Martin; Quandt, Thorsten (Hrsg.), Die neue Kommunikationswissenschaft. Theorien, Themen und Berufsfelder im Internet-Zeitalter. Eine Einführung. Wiesbaden: Westdeutscher Verlag, S. 71–87.

Behrends, T. (2001): Organisationskultur und Innovativität. Eine kulturtheoretische Analyse des Zusammenhangs zwischen sozialer Handlungsgrammatik und innovativem Organisationsverhalten, München: Rainer Hampp.

Bonfadelli, Heinz; Friemel, Thomas N.; Wirth, Werner (2010): Medienwirkungsforschung, in: Bonfadelli, Heinz; Jarren, Otfried; Siegert, Gabriele (Hrsg.): Einführung in die Publizistikwissenschaft. 3. Aufl. Bern: Haupt, S. 605–656.

Böhn, Andreas; Seidler, Andreas (2008): Mediengeschichte, Tübingen: Gunter Narr Verlag.

Brown, Tim (2008): Design Thinking, in: Harvard Business Review 6.2008, S. 84–96, URL: https://www.ideo.com/post/design-thinking-in-harvard-business-review, Abruf am 31.10.2019.

Dogruel, Leyla (2010): Die Bedeutung von Innovationen für die Analyse des Medienwandels. Vortrag auf dem Workshop „Medienentwicklung im Wandel" der DGPuK-Fachgruppe Soziologie der Medienkommunikation, 29.–30.10.2010, Hannover.

Dogruel, Leyla (2013): Eine Kommunikationswissenschaftliche Konzeption von Medieninnovation – Begriffsverständnisse und theoretische Zugänge, Wiesbaden: Springer Fachmedien.

Faßler, M.; Halbach, R. W. (1998): Einleitung in eine Mediengeschichte, in: Faßler, M.; Halbach, R. W. (Hrsg.): Geschichte der Medien, München: Fink, S. 17–52.

Faulstich, Werner (2004): Medientheorie, Mediengeschichte. in: Werner Faulstich (Hrsg.): Grundwissen Medien. 5. Aufl., München: Fink, S. 13–33.

Fröhlich, Kerstin (2010): Innovationssysteme der TV-Unterhaltungsproduktion, Komparative Analyse Deutschlands und Großbritanniens, Wiesbaden: GWV Fachverlage GmbH.

Garncarz, Joseph (2009): Kommunikation, Wissen, Unterhaltung – Ein Modell der Mediengeschichte. In Heinze, Thomas/ Lewinski-Reuter, Verena/ Steimle, Kerstin (Hrsg.): Innovation durch Kommunikation. Kommunikation als Innovationsfaktor für Organisationen. Wiesbaden: VS Verlag, S. 65–73.

Georges, Karl Ernst (1918): Ausführliches lateinisch-deutsches Handwörterbuch. Hannover 81918 (Nachdruck Darmstadt 1998), Band 2, Sp. 286, URL: http://www.zeno.org/nid/2000244626X, Abruf am 30.10.2019.

Grau, Oliver (2001): Telepräsenz. Zu Genealogie und Epistemologie von Interaktion und Simulation, In: Peter Gendolla (Hrsg.): Formen interaktiver Medienkunst: Geschichte, Tendenzen, Utopien, Suhrkamp: Frankfurt a. M., S. 39–63, URL: http://sammelpunkt.philo.at/579/1/Grau2.pdf, Abruf am 30.10.2019.

Grots, Alexander; Pratschke, Margarete (2009): Design Thinking – Kreativität als Methode, In: Marketing Review St. Gallen 2-2009, S. 18–23. URL: https://link.springer.com/article/10.1007/s11621-009-0027-4, Abruf am 31.10.2019.

Hauschildt, Jürgen; Salomo, Sören (2011) Innovationsmanagement 6. Auflage, Verlag Franz Vahlen, München, 2011.

Hemmerling, Marco (2014): Die Erweiterung der Architektur, in: Jeschke, Sabine; Kobbelt, Leif; Dröge, Alicia (Hrsg.): Exploring Virtuality, Wiesbaden: Springer Fachmedien, S. 111–132.

Hickethier, Knut (2012): Film und Fernsehanalyse, 5. Aufl., Stuttgart: J.B. Metzler Verlag.

Hofer, Matthias (2013): Präsenzerleben und Teleportation, in: Schweiger, Wolfgang; Fahr, Andreas (Hrsg.): Handbuch Medienwirkungsforschung, Wiesbaden: Springer Fachmedien, S. 279–294, URL: https://www.researchgate.net/publication/258332391_Prasenzerleben_und_Transportation, Download: https://doi.org/10.1007/978-3-531-18967-3_14, Abruf am 31.10.2019.

Karnowski, Veronika (2013): Diffusionstheorie, in: Schweiger, Wolfgang; Fahr, Andreas (Hrsg.): Handbuch Medienwirkungsforschung, Wiesbaden: Springer Fachmedien, S. 513–528.

Kiefer, Marie Luise (2001): Medienökonomik, Einführung in eine ökonomische Theorie der Medien. München: De Gruyter Oldenbourg.

Klimmt, Christoph; Hartmann, Tilo; Vorderer, Peter (2005): Macht der Neuen Medien? Überwältigung und kritische Rezeptionshaltung in virtuellen Medienumgebungen. in Publizistik 50. Jahrgang, H.4: 422–437.

Küng, Lucy (2008): Innovation and Creativity in the Media Industry: What? Where? How? In Dal Zotto, Cinzia/ van Kranenburg, Hans (Hrsg.): Management and Innovation in the Media Industry. Cheltenham, UK: Edward Elgar: 3–13.

Lanier, Jaron, Virtual Environments and Interactivity: Windows to the Future, in: SIGGRAPH Panel Proceedings, Boston 1989. Pages 7–18 ISBN:0-89791-353-1, URL: http://dl.acm.org/citation.cfm?doid=77276.77278; Download doi > https://doi.org/10.1145/77276.77278, Abruf am 31.10.2019.

Löffelholz, Martin; Quandt Thorsten (2003): Kommunikationswissenschaften im Wandel, in: Löffelholz, Martin; Quandt, Thorsten (Hrsg.): Die neue Kommunikationswissenschaft. Theorien, Themen und Berufsfelder im Internet-Zeitalter, Eine Einführung, Wiesbaden: Westdeutscher Verlag, S. 13–42.

McLuhan, Marshall (1964): Understanding Media, Extention of Man, S. 1–18, URL: http://web.mit.edu/allanmc/www/mcluhan.mediummessage.pdf, Abruf am 31.10.2019.

Metzinger, Thomas; Madary, Michael (19.02.2016): Real Virtuality: A Code of Ethical Conduct. Recommendations for Good Scientific Practice and the Consumers of VR Technology, in *Frontiers in Robotics and AI*, URL: http://journal.frontiersin.org/article/10.3389/frobt.2016.00003/full, Download: https://doi.org/10.3389/frobt.2016.00003, Abruf am 31.10.2019.

Ommeln, Miriam (2008): Erkenntnistheorie im Virtuellen. Nietzscheforschung, Band 15 (JG), S. 95–112, URL: https://www.philosophie.kit.edu/downloads/Ommeln_Erkenntnistheorie_im_Virtuellen.pdf, Abruf am 31.10.2019.

Rittmann, Tim (2008): MMORPGs als virtuelle Welten – Immersion und Repräsentation, Boizenburg: Verlag Werner Hülsbusch.

Rogers, Everett M. (2003): Diffusion of Innovations (5th ed.) New York: Free Press.

Saxer, Ulrich (1999): Der Forschungsgegenstand der Medienwissenschaft. in Leonhard, Joachim-Felix/ Ludwig, Hans-Werner/ Schwarze, Dietrich et al. (Hrsg.): Medienwissenschaft. Ein Handbuch zur Entwicklung der Medien und Kommunikationsformen. Berlin u. a.: de Gruyter: S. 1–14.

Schmidt, S. J. (1994): Die Wirklichkeit des Beobachters. In: Merten/ Schmidt/ Weischenberg (Hrsg.): Die Wirklichkeit der Medien. Opladen: Westdeutscher, S. 3–14.

Schmidt, Siegfried J, (2000): Kalte Faszination – Medien. Kultur Wissenschaft in der Mediengesellschaft, Weilerswist: Velbrück Wissenschaft.

Scholze-Stubenrecht, Werner et al. (2006): Duden: Die deutsche Rechtschreibung, 24. Aufl., Bd. 1, Mannheim: Dudenverlag, Bibliographisches Institut & F.A. Brockhaus.

Schumpeter, J. A. (1912) Theorie der wirtschaftlichen Entwicklung, Leipzig, Verlag von Duncker & Humblot. 1912. URL: https://link.springer.com/chapter/10.1007%2F0-306-48082-4_2, Abruf am 31.10.2019.

Schumpeter, J. A. (1961): Konjunkturzyklen: eine theoretische, historische und statistische Analyse des kapitalistischen Prozesses, Bd. 1. Göttingen: Vandenhoeck & Ruprecht.

Slater, Mel; Sanchez-Vives, Maria V. (2016): Enhancing Our Live with Immersive Virtual Reality in Front. Robot. AI, 19.12.2016, URL: http://journal.frontiersin.org/article/10.3389/frobt.2016.00074/full, Download: https://doi.org/10.3389/frobt.2016.00074, Abruf am 31.10.2019.

Stähler, Patrick (2001): Dissertation, Geschäftsmodelle in der digitalen Ökonomie, 2. Auflage, St. Gallen (2001), URL:https://www.researchgate.net/publication/35493106_Geschaftsmodelle_in_der_digitalen_Okonomie_Merkmale_Strategien_und_Auswirkungen, Abruf 04.11.2019.

Steger, Johannes (10.7.2017): Eine Revolution auf Standby, Handelsblatt, URL: http://www.handelsblatt.com/my/unternehmen/it-medien/virtual-reality-eine-revolution-auf-standby/v_detail_tab_print/20037106.html, Abruf am 31.10.2019.

Uhrig, Meike (2015): Darstellung, Rezeption und Wirkung von Emotionen im Film – eine inter-disziplinäre Studie, Wiesbaden: Springer Fachmedien.

Vahs, Dietmar; Buhrmester, Ralf (2002): Innovationsmanagement, Stuttgart: Schäffer-Poeschel.

Vere (2010): URL: http://www.vereproject.eu, Abruf am 10.9.2017.

Witmer, Bob G.; Singer, Michael J. (1998): Measuring Presence in Virtual Environments: A Presence; Questionnaire. Presence: Teleoperators and Virtual Environments 7, S. 225–240, URL: https://nil.cs.uno.edu/publications/papers/witmer1998measuring.pdf, Abruf am 31.10.2019.

Wolling, Jens; Kuhlmann, Christoph (2003): Das Internet als Gegenstand und Instrument der empirischen Kommunikationsforschung, in: Löffelholz, Martin; Quandt, Thorsten (Hrsg.), Die neue Kommunikationswissenschaft. Theorien, Themen und Berufsfelder im Internet-Zeitalter. Eine Einführung. Wiesbaden: Westdeutscher Verlag: S. 131–161.

User Experience and Needs

5

Those who know people's emotions and perceptual processes can tell the best stories.

This chapter focuses on the media user, his or her media use needs and his or her media experience. The aim is to use specific needs and experiences to identify motives that encourage a user to engage with media in general and with AR and VR in particular. The term user refers to a user of, for example, a digital product (cf. Lackes and Siepermann 2017). Media studies refer to media users as recipients, audiences or viewers, while computer science refers to them as users. Since the reception and use of media is a communicative process and interaction is a specific feature of AR and VR, the media user is uniformly referred to as user in this thesis, who is either active or passive (cf. Hickethier 2012, pp. 6, 9 f.). The analysis of the user takes place from two perspectives.

The investigation of motives for media use is part of the research on media effects. Investigation of motives for media use is the first perspective. Communication science deals with the user and asks why and in what way he uses media. In this context, psychological and sociological motives are examined that trigger the willingness to act to use media (cf. Schweiger and Fahr 2013, p. 10; Bonfadelli et al. 2010, p. 610).

The reception of media and the experience of media content form the second perspective. Reception research is part of communication science as well as media and cultural studies. Media studies focus more on the creation and impact of content and aesthetics, which has an influence on media reception (cf. Gehrau 2013, p. 596; Hickethier 2012, p. 27). Reception is understood as the emotional and cognitive process of understanding in the recipient while watching a medium such as a film. This communicative process is influenced by cultural and personal experiences and leads to individual interpretations of

E. Langer, *Media Innovations AR and VR*, https://doi.org/10.1007/978-3-662-66280-9_5

the viewed medium (cf. Hickethier 2012, pp. 4, 6). Since AR and VR integrate interactive and audiovisual media and the media effect plays a special role in AR and VR, both perspectives are appropriate.

In Sect. 5.1, user needs and forms of media use are examined and supplemented with findings from usability research and innovation development. This is based on the assumption that specific user needs can provide indications of success factors and that appropriate methods are used to identify these needs.

The investigation of the user experience and reception of media content is of particular importance for VR and AR, since the media have a reality-changing effect on the user. In Sect. 5.2, the media effect phenomena of presence experience and transportation are applied to AR and VR and examined for success factors that fulfil a user need.

5.1   User Needs of Media Use

Media and communication studies assume that media use fundamentally serves to satisfy needs and that users experience a reward through the way in which they use media (cf. Bonfadelli 2004, p. 4). A need is generally described as a feeling, wish or desire for something or someone (cf. Stangl 2017).

5.1.1   Need for Reward

According to the uses-and-gratifications approach of Elihu Katz et al. needs are multidimensional. In their Israel study, Katz et al. identified 35 user needs. According to their assumption, turning to a specific medium is a need satisfaction that is associated with a reward from which the user benefits. This assumes that media use does not happen automatically, but is an active and purposeful social action on the part of the user, behind which is the motive of benefit and reward. Depending on the need, the user determines whether and how to turn to the medium or media content (cf. Bonfadelli 2004, p. 4). Katz et al. divided the 35 identified user needs into four categories of media use needs.

Cognitive needs refer to the desire for knowledge and information.

This refers to the understanding and satisfaction of curiosity, but also to the desire for self-awareness and the creation of meaning through media use.

Affective needs are the desire for entertainment, relaxation, distraction. Media use is used for stimulation and distraction, to escape from everyday life (escapism).

Social-interactive needs correspond to the desire for social recognition and contact. Media use is intended to offer topics for conversation or to replace the function of missing conversation partners, such as talk shows or chat rooms.

Integrative-habitual needs stem from the desire for trust-building media use that is integrated as a ritual into the daily routine and structures it (cf. Bonfadelli et al. 2010, p. 622 f.; Bonfadelli 2004, p. 7 f.; Katz et al. 1973, p. 5 in pdf).

The user consciously decides according to his need which medium represents a reward (gratification) for him. The uses-and-gratification approach is the basis of surveys on the usage behaviour of mass media. In this method, user needs are derived on the basis of media use, such as "I use the program for entertainment" or "Because it is part of the habit". These statements are assigned to corresponding media (cf. Bonfadelli et al. 2010, p. 622 f.). The reward approach assumes that the user knows his need and consciously chooses a medium. Bonfadelli criticizes that on the basis of such research methods statements are made about usage needs for which media offers are developed. Through quota measurement and subsequent user surveys, need and offer confirm each other (cf. Bonfadelli et al. 2010, p. 625). Nevertheless, the uses-and-gratification approach is considered the standard model of media use research (cf. Uhrig 2015, p. 67; Hasebrink 2003, p. 114).

The four need categories of the uses-and-gratification approach provide a basis for examining the user need for media use of AR and VR. For example, a cognitive need gratification for information when using AR and VR would be the media-specific feature of obtaining a hidden information about a place. The reward for media use would be learning about new places through experiential information. This example shows that a location-specific media experience is not considered in the use-and-graphication approach. Nevertheless, the approach has relevance because the method is used in media use research.

5.1.2   Information and Entertainment Needs

The media scientist Knut Hickethier assumes that users[1] have a fundamental need for entertainment and information, which they satisfy through their choice of media content (cf. Hickethier 2012, p. 213). Hickethier's focus is on the media content of film and television. The theoretical basis is Werner Früh's Triadic-Dynamic Entertainment Theory, which is understood as a framing theory. According to Früh, the entertainment experience of watching television is created by a process of states during reception (dynamic approach). The prerequisite is that "personal, medial and situational or social factors [transactional approach] are compatible and the recipient also has the certainty of sovereign control over the situation" (Wünsch 2006, p. 95, cited in Früh et al. 2002, p. 240). According to this, the need for entertainment and information arises less from the need to use media than from the individual life situation. The desire for entertainment and information is thus dependent on the needs and life situation of a user. This is based on the assumption that the user wants to be told certain stories that provide emotional stimulation. Through the stimulation of the content, the user experiences a "sensual gain in experience" (Hickethier 2012, p. 213). At the same time, through the comparison between the story and the reflection on one's own life situation, the content offers a differentiation, which amounts to the affirmation of one's own way of life. The gratification is the stabilization of one's life situation.

---

[1] Hickethier uses the term spectator at this point. The term is replaced with the term user.

This simple description is based on complex affective and cognitive processes of information processing, which influence the user's perception process through camera perspective and equipment (cf. Wünsch 2006, p. 130). Hickethier points out that the viewer is "not primarily interested in media innovations" (Hickethier 2012, p. 213), but in traditional forms of storytelling as these promote the entertainment experience.

With regard to AR and VR, the assumption can be made that new types of media offerings can satisfy entertainment and information needs through AR and VR, which represent stabilization in distinction to one's own life. According to Hickethier's assumption, these have a higher acceptance if they fall back on familiar narrative modes (cf. Hickethier 2012, p. 213).

5.1.3   Need for Stimulation

The mood management theory was developed in the context of entertainment research by the emotional psychologist Dolf Zillmann, who investigates the entertainment and excitement experience of media content. According to his theory, the motivation of media use is a stimulation need for entertainment and excitement (cf. Trepte 2013, p. 101). Dolf Zillmann et al. assume an unconscious motivation of media use in the user, who aims to experience mood elevation. The theory was tested in 1984 in the Selective Exposure Experiment by Zillmann and Jennings Bryant (cf. Reinicke 2016; Uhrig 2015, p. 68).

According to Zillmann's theory, media use unconsciously serves stimulation. The need for stimulation is shaped by the situational state of the user (cf. Hasebrink 2003, p. 115; Uhrig 2015, p. 69). The affect that media content has on the user changes their mood. The term affect used in emotional impact research refers to a physiological arousal such as sweating and heartbeat, while the emotion-specific approach of affect is understood as emotions such as anger, disgust, etc. (cf. Wirth 2013, p. 229). Zillmann names four factors according to which media content can be classified: as stimulating and non-stimulating or relaxing and boring. The affect on the user depends on the emotion-stimulating quality of the media content (cf. Uhrig 2015, p. 70).

To investigate the reception effect of media content in AR and VR, the need for an experience for stimulation purposes could be examined.

Since AR and VR are interactive audiovisual media, the aspect of interactivity would have to be included. A critical challenge is that the mood management theory, like the uses-and-gratification approach, only queries user needs during or after media use. To determine success factors for AR and VR applications, a consideration of user needs in the development phase would be relevant.

5.2   Identification of User Needs

In the following, methods are presented that already take user needs into account during the production of content. In addition, aspects of interactivity and space are integrated. Both are media-specific characteristics of AR and VR. The application of the methods can provide indications of media-specific needs.

5.2.1   Design Thinking

Design Thinking is a method with which products, services and innovations can be developed and optimized. Design is the English term for creation, the German equivalent for the English word thinking is denken (cf. Messinger et al. 1997, p. 309, 1223). The product is developed from the user's perspective. Decisive for the success of the method are multidisciplinary teams, a flexible space and an iterative process. The process proceeds through the six phases of understanding, observing, finding a point of view, developing an idea, prototyping and testing, through which rapid product development is possible. The teams visualize their ideas and develop personas as user types based on the findings. For this, user-specific needs, such as values and attitudes, are integrated. Ideas are developed for these personas and turned into simple prototypes. Rapid user tests produce new results and contribute to optimization (cf. Grots and Pratschke 2009, pp. 18–23; Brown 2008, pp. 84–96).

5.2.2   UX Design

The German equivalent of user experience is Nutzererlebnis or Nutzererfahrung (cf. Messinger et al. 1997, pp. 1305, 406). The abbreviation UX stands for user experience. UX design is therefore the design of the user's experience with a product. The method is used for the development of complex interactive products that require user guidance. Space-related and user-specific aspects such as needs and expectations are included (cf. Thesmann 2016, pp. 2, 8). Therefore, UX design is also a relevant method for a design thinking process. In UX design, the user experience is understood as a holistic process that integrates aesthetic, emotional and cognitive aspects of a user experience and takes the entire perception process into account. The user's location is also included (cf. Thesmann 2016, p. 44 f.) To determine needs, user scenarios (costumer journey) are developed on the basis of personas, which are visualized in storyboards and prototypes (cf. Thesmann 2016, p. 277).

The two user-centered approaches design thinking and UX design take into account an individual user perspective. This is relevant in relation to AR and VR in that it involves interactive and audiovisual content in a three-dimensional medium. Fulfilling a user need could satisfy the desire for interactivity in content and space or the desire for passivity. This example makes it clear that media use depends on individual needs, types of use and user types.[2]

5.2.3   Summary of User Needs

The models for the study of media use presented in Sect. 5.1 introduce the motives for use on the basis of needs and gratifications. Needs are interpreted in different ways. The use-and-gratification approach offers four categories of needs according to which a specific form of media use rewards the user. A basic need for information and entertainment is assumed. Mood management theory focuses on stimulation through media entertainment and excitement gratification. The three models are united by the desire for need satisfaction through media stimulation and reward. They provide a basis for identifying user needs. Need satisfaction through a spatial or interactive experience is missing and would need to be methodologically developed for application to AR and VR.

These aspects as well as user-specific needs are already integrated in the methods of design thinking and UX design during product development. It can be assumed that knowledge of methods for developing user experiences for VR and AR applications contributes to success. This aspect is queried in the expert interviews.

5.3   User Experience in VR and AR

The media definition of AR and VR in Sect. 4.3 identified the specific characteristics of presence experience, space and the user being physically present in the medium. In combination, these criteria form a unique selling point of AR and VR. This phenomenon can be summarized as the phenomenon of presence experience, which integrates the user- and space-related category.

In the following chapter, the concepts of presence experience and transportation are introduced and applied to VR and AR. This is based on the assumption that intensive presence experience is a success factor for AR and VR applications.

---

[2] This paper does not deal with user typologies as this aspect was not asked about in the expert interviews. User types would, however, be able to provide relevant information about success factors as user typologies reveal individual needs, for example on the basis of the Sinus-Milieu model. This groups people into ten social groups based on similar attitudes to life, such as values and economic living conditions. Each group is distinguished by specific characteristics (cf. Flaig and Marc 2017, p. 6 f.). The characteristics allow conclusions to be drawn about needs for which specific offers for AR and VR applications can be developed.

5.3.1   Presence Experience and Transportation

Cultural studies, educational sciences, psychology and engineering offer several studies on the phenomenon of immersion in a medium. The terms range from immersion, telepresence and presence experience to transportation. The disparate terms have been developed from the respective sciences and describe the phenomenon of media merging (cf. Hofer 2013, p. 280 f.) For this work, the two terms presence experience and transportation are placed in the foreground and applied to AR and VR.

5.3.2   Definitions

Presence experience is a feature of AR and VR and describes a psychological concept that creates a perceptual illusion through the perception of being in the virtual environment into which the user is immersed (cf. Hofer 2013, p. 282; Schuemie et al. 2001, p. 184 f.).

In this context the term immersion is also used to describe a physical or psychological feeling of immersion in an environment that gives the user the feeling of leaving the real world and being "present" only in the virtual environment (cf. Sadowski and Stanney 2002). The concepts of presence experience and immersion are similar. For Witmer and Singer immersion is not an experiential category, but a measurable stimulus property that describes being enclosed and interacting in a virtual environment created by a constant stream of stimuli and experiences. The enhancement of this is the experience of presence (cf. Witmer and Singer 1998, p. 227).

In media and communication studies the term presence experience is applied to all media, since the spatial presence experience occurs during the reception of all media (cf. Hartmann et al. 2005, p. 21). A term used in this context is transportation. This term is used in film and media studies. It is based on Gerrig's (1993) transportation theory, which describes being transported "into a narrative world" (Hofer 2013, p. 282) and is generated by the reception of a medium (cf. Gerrig 1993, pp. 4, 10). The journey is integrated in the concept of transportation.

The phenomena immersion, presence experience and transportation are united by the concept of immersion in a medium as well as the perceived change of location without a real physical change of place. For this paper only presence experience and transportation are considered in more detail and applied to the two media VR and AR.

5.3.3   Dimensions of Presence Experience and Transportation

Presence experience and transportation are psychological constructs based on concepts of media effects. The basic assumption is that presence experience and transportation arise from the user's shift of attention towards the medium. Users block out the real-physical reality, which gives them the feeling that they are in the place mediated by the medium.

Unlike presence experience, transportation has an additional narrative component that makes the user, through shift of attention towards the medium, travel to the place of the narrative (cf. Hofer 2013, pp. 283, 287). All of the user's mental resources are focused on the events of the narrative (cf. Green and Brock 2000, pp. 3 f.). With their research on narrative persuasion, Melanie C. Green and Timothy C. Brock have refined Gerrig's transportation theory. According to them, transportation is the complete merging of attention (cognitive engagement), imagination (mental imagery), and emotion (affective engagement) with the medium (cf. Appel et al. 2015, p. 4; Hofer 2013, p. 283).[3] In the case of intense presence experience and transportation, the user feels present in the place. In doing so, he has the perception that the medium itself is dissolving. Schubert describes presence experience as a "cognitive feeling, [...] as a consciously perceived event of unconsciously occurring processes" (Hofer 2013, p. 292, in brackets in the original).

5.4   Emergence of Presence Experience and Transportation

Several factors are necessary for the emergence of presence experience and transportation in the user, which essentially comprise the localization of a person in the media space and his perceptual processes, quasi a first-person perspective in the media space. Four factors are necessary for the user to feel present in the medium: content properties of the media space, cognitive properties, personality properties on the user's side, and narrative properties (cf. Wünsch 2006, p. 73; Hofer 2013, p. 284 f.; Witmer and Singer 1998, p. 228).

5.4.1   Prerequisite Media Properties

A high number of interaction possibilities and their closeness to reality contribute to the emergence of the experience of presence. If stimulating media content such as camera perspective, sound and haptics as well as physical action are added, these increase the experience of presence[4] (cf. Hofer 2013, p. 284; Witmer and Singer 1998, p. 229).

Narrative factors that have a narrative function in the representation and function in the media space further promote the emergence of presence experience, especially when a narrative completely fills the entire media space with actors, objects and events. In addition, social elements, such as group experiences, contribute to the user's feeling of being

---

[3] Green and Brock were able to empirically prove the effect of blending through their Transportation Scale (cf. Hofer 2013, p. 283, footnote). Their measurement method quantifies user experience and is used for narrative persuasion research. The research medium was a narrative in written form (cf. Appel and Richter 2010, p. 103).

[4] The study by Martin Usoh et al. shows that walking naturally in a VR application, compared to an application without body movement, increases the experience of presence (cf. Dörner et al. 2013, p. 171; Usoh et al. 1999, p. 359 f.).

in the place (cf. Hofer 2013, p. 284; Schuemie et al. 2001, pp. 184, 191 f.). In this context, the naturalness of the objects, the interaction possibilities and the environment are attributed an important role in the creation of the experience of presence.

5.4.2 The Attention of the User

In order for the user to experience presence, he must engage with the medium. For VR and AR applications, this means turning to the 360° space and its content via a display. This implies a conscious decision on the part of the user to devote his attention to the medium and to willingly shift his perception from the real physical environment to the virtual and virtually augmented environment. This perceptual shift is what Witmer et al. call involvement, which also works for other media (cf. Witmer and Singer 1998, p. 227). Only the cognitive process of shifting the user's attention to the medium can give rise to the experience of presence and transportation. According to Green and Brock, the process is supported by the user's imagination or mental imagery (cf. Appel et al. 2015, p. 4, Hofer 2013, p. 283). Neuroscientist Antonio Damasio defines mental imagery as internal or mental images that generate neural traces that can be retrieved when needed (cf. Damasio 2010, p. 28). This means that the mental images and inner pictures contribute to whether the user feels present in the media space.

5.4.2.1 User Emotions

Emotional factors are the third competency that are important in the creation of presence experience. These are divided into two components, the personality traits of a user and the emotional guidance of the narrative. The following excursus on emotional processes should help to better understand user experiences in VR and AR.

5.4.2.2 Definitions of Emotions

The term emotion is used inconsistently as various theories from emotion research exist. For this thesis the concept of emotion is considered from the perspectives of communication and film studies and the neuroscientist Antonio Damasio, in order to explore the parts emotions play in the experience of presence and transportation.

According to Damasio, emotions are complex processes that run mostly automatically in the body and trigger basic emotions such as disgust, anger, joy, fear, love, lust. They are designed to perform an action when needed, such as fleeing in the case of fear or laughing in the case of joy. In doing so the processes are supported by a cognitive program that makes evaluations (cf. Damasio 2010, pp. 122, 123). Emotions are "generated by images of objects or events that are happening at this moment or have happened in the past [...]" (Damasio 2010, p. 124). While according to Damasio emotions are driven by ways of thinking and experiences, feelings are the composite perceptions of all mental and physical processes. Damasio assumes that the course of emotional reaction chains is a cycle that begins in the brain (cf. Damasio 2010, p. 123 f.). According to his assumption, emotional experiences are stored in the body, the brain has a cartography of the body and is thus able to simulate certain physical states (cf. Damasio 2010, p. 113 f.). This aspect is relevant in relation to bodily perception in an AR and VR application, in which experiences can be stored or retrieved in this way.

In media effects research, on the other hand, emotions are understood as affects that arise through media use. All theoretical approaches assume that the reception of media content triggers physiological states of arousal in the autonomic nervous system, which generate moods and emotional states in the form of emotions or affects (cf. Wirth 2013, pp. 228, 231; Uhrig 2015, p. 69 f.).

As a third component user-specific emotions thus contribute significantly to the generation of presence experience and transportation. On the user level the individual need for emotions plays a central role, which is different for each user. According to the findings of Appel and Richter, the need for emotions is anchored in the personality of the individual. In an experiment designed to investigate an increase in the intensity of transportation through positive emotional media content, Appel and Richter were able to prove that participants with a pronounced need for emotion experienced more intense transportation than participants with a low need for emotion (cf. Appel and Richter 2010, p. 123 f.).[5] Emotional needs are coupled with stimulation through entertainment and excitement by means of a medium. In this context the effect of the spatial displacement of one's own location from the real physical world into a virtually media-mediated world, the fact of being transported itself, can have a high entertainment potential (cf. Hofer 2013, p. 289; Green et al. 2004). The art of entertainment and excitement lies in the varied orchestration of emotional modes (cf. Grodal 1999, p. 132). Since emotional stimulation according to mood management theory presupposes the need for entertainment and excitement, it can be assumed that the stimulation of arousal states with AR and VR is desired if the content promises this (cf. Section 5.1.3).

5.4.3   Narrative Emotion Control

The experience of presence and transportation are concepts that are consciously used in film and theatre, where transportation is created through the story. The reception of theatre and cinema films has a long history of development, which has been developed and learned by producers and users alike. Film studies distinguish between every day and film emotions (cf. Uhrig 2015, p. 36; Platinga 2009, p. 79). Unlike in real-physical everyday life, where a selection is filtered out of a multitude of stimuli, the user's emotions are guided in film. This is done through emotional cues in the film, which have an emotion-triggering effect on the viewer through dramaturgy, actors, film editing and music. The user experiences the film emotionally, but knows that what they are seeing is not real, such as when

---

[5]The narrative content presented in the experiment was available to participants in text form.

watching horror films (cf. Uhrig 2015, p. 36; Carroll 1990; Eder 2007, p. 655).[6] The ideas or imaginings generated by the film are perceived as real emotions. The brain retrieves stored mental imagery in the body and reassembles it during the imagination through matching and highlighting. Damasio describes this as "attempts to return to a past reality" (Damasio 2010, p. 162).

Unlike in a cinema seat in front of a screen, in a VR or AR application the user is directly in the scene in a virtual or virtually augmented space. There he will follow his impulses and either observe the scene, look at the environment or interact with elements. Directing emotions with classic movie cues in a 360° spatial perspective is difficult. The brain does not yet have any conceptual images of how image montages look and feel when spaces change in which the user is physically located.

Presumably, this film technology, which is being developed since 100 years, will not use the same dramaturgical effects as a film projected on a two-dimensional screen. This aspect is relevant for the investigation of success factors, since the experience of presence and transportation require new stylistic devices and narrative forms. In addition, there is the role of human representation in a virtual environment. On the one hand, this triggers the learned perceptual processes in the user during film reception; on the other hand, users perceive the three-dimensionality and physical presence of their self in the space. This triggers the same emotional processes as a real physical environment (cf. Damasio 2010, pp. 114, 116, 164).

It is the goal of an AR and VR application to increase the intensity of experience of presence and transportation. Thus, the need for a spatial experience through presence experience and transportation can be identified at the user's need level. These aspects must be queried using the categories in the expert interviews.

5.4.4   Summary

From the description of presence experience and transportation it becomes clear that a naturalness of the media content and its emotional stimulation are fundamentally involved in the emergence and enhancement of presence experience and transportation. The prerequisite is that the user turns his attention to the medium. This willingness depends on user needs and personality traits, for example the desire for emotion. Multisensory content increases the experience of presence and transportation, so that the change to the media-mediated location can be experienced in a more immediate and real way. Transferred to immersive media such as AR and VR, the experiential power of these media becomes

---

[6] Jens Eder assumes that sensory stimuli generate emotions in the viewer and influence perception. Eder has written an extensive work on emotion guidance through narration (cf. Uhrig 2015, pp. 15, 39 f.; Jens Eder 2007). Carroll and Russel deal with emotion cues and have developed a circumplex model according to which emotions are dimensioned in their opposites (cf. Uhrig 2015, p. 34; Carroll 1990, p. 6).

clear. In AR, the experience of the real physical place contributes to the experience of presence.[7]

5.5   Experience of Presence in the Room

The following section considers the media-specific feature of the space of AR and VR in terms of presence experience, transportation, and user experience.

Space and displacement are central features of the experience of presence and transportation. Both concepts are studied in media and cultural studies. For this thesis, sociological aspects such as spatial design and architecture are also considered. These should give clues to success factors for spatial design and user experience in virtual and virtually extended spaces.

5.5.1   Experience of Space

People are used to living in spaces. They fulfil functional and emotional purposes. They create systems of orientation and rules in the form of signs that help them cope with everyday life and influence their perception of their surroundings. According to sociologist Nina Baur, perceiving a space means not yet knowing how to use it. She refers to the experience of urban planning and sociological studies of spatial appropriation of children and adolescents by Ahrend and Herlyn et al., according to which people make space their own in a socialization process, shaped by their ideas of space based on principles and needs. To this end people develop specific interaction practices with objects and furnishings. In this process, the use is individual and not always in the sense of the designers (cf. Baur 2013; Herlyn et al. 2003, pp. 15 f., 112 f., 218 f.; Ahrend 2002, pp. 34 f., 69 f.).

The design of spaces is a constant creation of media spaces, the goal of which, from a cultural and media studies perspective, is an expansion of reality. AR and VR continue this tradition with their own technical possibilities (cf. Section 3.1). Following McLuhan's concept of media, according to which every object is understood as a medium, real-physical spaces have the same communicative effect as artificially created spaces (cf. Sect. 4.2.3). They consist of semiotic systems that express themselves in architecture and unfold their narrative power on the user as in cathedrals or mega cities. An architectural experience is expressed in the way that the effect of a building influences the recipient's space. Gutzmer refers to the discourse of media theory in architecture, according to which it is attributed the function of a social assignment (cf. Grutzmer 2015, pp. 21, 28). For the British sociologists Scott Lash and Celia Lury, buildings "themselves become a medium – and thus also a venue for communicative processes" (Grutzmer 2015, p. 29 f., cited in

---

[7] Statements in the expert interviews indicate that the experience of presence in both immersive media AR and VR is dependent on the screen.

Lash 2002, p. 149; Lury 2007, p. 36). Accordingly, the Burj Kalifa in Dubai, currently the tallest building, would be a medium. Its shape and height give the building a symbolic meaning of grandeur that can be evaluated as power and makes the viewer forget that he is actually in an artificially built environment of architectural visions in the middle of the Dubai desert. Buildings are thus virtual extensions of reality. The reception of the overall composition is not perceived by the recipient as an extension of physical reality. The reason is that the semiotic effect of the signs and objects are learned and internalized by the recipient through the constant use of this medium. They are perceived as familiar by the recpient through repetition. Sociologist Daniel Kahneman calls this the human brain's pursuit of coherence, seeking patterns from the past after associations in the process of understanding and creating causal connections. It is a laziness of the brain that favors cognitive ease over cognitive strain (see Kahneman 2011, pp. 83, 100). Damasio describes the process as a matching of external "signals from the [internal] images representing a particular object [...] can trigger very specific emotional chain reactions" (Damasio 2010, p. 125). Through haptic stimuli, such as the heat in Dubai, and through the particular aesthetics of the building, the viewer's perception is influenced and matched with emotions and experiences stored in the body. This process can therefore be compared to the emotional processes of presence experience and transportation, where cognitive (visual impression, heat] and emotional factors (semiotics and personal characteristics) change the perception of space (cf. Section 5.4). Space, as the living space of people, has a central role in reality, virtuality and presence experience for the localization of the user himself.

In relation to the design of interactive virtual and virtually extended spaces, it is therefore about more than just a human-machine interface (user interface design). Therefore, communicative needs, physiological, psychological as well as design aspects have to be taken into account, which contribute to the creation of presence experience and transportation. A realistic familiar environment seems to play an important role as it influences the emotional user experience and narration.

5.6   Conclusion

In this chapter, the user level of AR and VR applications was examined in order to identify categories based on user needs of media use and the user experience, which provide indications of success factors. User needs can therefore lie in the knowledge of the methods presented in Sections 5.1 and 5.2. It was identified that the real physical space as well as the interaction in relation to user needs are hardly considered in the presented methods. Spatial perception is therefore of particular importance in two respects, once through three-dimensional media use and through three-dimensional media experience. The latter was presented in Sect. 5.3 on the basis of the media effect phenomena of presence experience and transportation. It became clear that the emotional perception of audiovisual

Table 5.1 Overview of the categories user experiences and needs

Categories	Subcategories
Content	Media format, story, three-dimensionality space and content, Interaction and communication, linking space and content
Users	Three-dimensional user experience of media use, interaction and communication, three-dimensional space and body experience
Economics	Production and production method
	Economic and structural framework conditions

Brief overview of the categories from this chapter (source: own representation)

media and spatial perception generate similar affects in the user. Both contribute to the generation and enhancement of the experience of presence and transportation.

Accordingly, presence experience and transportation represent a unique media experience of VR and AR, which must be created for the user. At the user's level of need, the desire for three-dimensional, perception-changing media experiences can be assumed. In this context familiar narrative forms, realistic representations and natural interaction and communication seem to have a positive effect. The success factors that contribute positively to the experience of presence and transportation will be asked in the expert interviews.

This extends the **user category** with the **user experience of** media use, **spatial experience, physical experience** and **interaction and communication** in the subcategories. These are examined for success factors, which user needs must be fulfilled, which contribute positively to the presence experience and the transportation (Table 5.1).

Literature

Ahrend, Christine (2002): Mobilitätsstrategien zehnjähriger Jungen und Mädchen als Grundlage städtischer Verkehrsplanung. Münster/München: Waxmann. S. 34–53, 69–11, 144–158, 197–206.

Appel, Markus; Richter, Tobias; Green, Melanie C. et al. (2015): The Transportation Scale-Short Form (TS-SF), in Media Psychology URL: https://www.researchgate.net/publication/267980054_The_Transportation_Scale-Short_Form_TS-SF, Download: https://doi.org/10.1080/15213269.2014.987400, Abruf am 31.10.2019.

Appel, Markus; Richter, Tobias (2010): Transportation and Need for Affect in Narrative Persuasion: A Mediated Moderation Model; in Media Psychology, URL: https://www.researchgate.net/publication/259970610_Transportation_and_Need_for_Affect_in_Narrative_Persuasion_A_Mediated_Moderation_Model, Download: https://doi.org/10.1080/1521326100379984, Abruf am 31.10.2019.

Baur, Nina (21.03.2013): Die Interaktion von Mensch und Raum durch Raumproduktion, Raumwahrnehmung und Raumaneignung, SozBlog der Deutschen Gesellschaft für Soziologie (DGS), URL: http://blog.soziologie.de/?s=Die+Interaktion+von+Mensch+und+Raum+durch+Raumproduktion%2C+Raumwahrnehmung+und+Raumaneignung, Abruf am 31.10.2019.

Bonfadelli, Heinz (2004): Neue Perspektiven: Medienzuwendung als soziales Handeln, in Medienwirkungsforschung I. Grundlagen, 3. Aufl., Konstanz: UVK Verlagsgesellschaft mbH, S. 167–207.

Bonfadelli, Heinz; Friemel, Thomas N.; Wirth, Werner (2010): Medienwirkungsforschung, in: Bonfadelli, Heinz; Jarren, Otfried; Siegert, Gabriele (Hrsg.): Einführung in die Publizistikwissenschaft. 3. Aufl. Bern: Haupt, S. 605–656.

Brown, Tim (2008): Design Thinking, in: Harvard Business Review 6.2008, S. 84–96, URL: https://www.ideo.com/post/design-thinking-in-harvard-business-review, Abruf am 31.10.2019.

Flaig, Berthold-Bodo, Calmbach Marc (2017): Informationen zu den Sinus Milieus 2017, Sinus Institut, URL: https://www.sinus-institut.de/veroeffentlichungen/downloads/download-a/searchresult/download-c/Category/, Abruf am 31.10.2019.

Carroll, Noel (1990): The philosophy of horror. Or: Paradoxes of the heart, New York/London: Routledge.

Damasio, Antonio (2010): Selbst ist der Mensch – Körper, Geist und die Entstehung des menschlichen Bewusstseins, München: Siedler-Verlag.

Dörner, Ralf et al. (2013): Einleitung, in: Dörner, Ralf; Broll, Wolfgang; Grimm, Pau; Jung, Bernhard (Hrsg.): Virtual und Augmented Reality (VR/AR), Heidelberg: Springer, S. 1–31.

Eder, Jens (2007): Gefühle im Widerstreit, A Clockwork Orange und die Erklärung audiovisueller Emotionen, in: Bartsch, Anne; Eder, Jens; Fahlenbrach, Kathrin (Hrsg.): Audiovisuelle Emotionen. Emotionsdarstellung und Emotionsvermittlung durch audiovisuelle Medienangebote, Köln: Halem-Verlag, S. 256–276.

Früh, Werner; Schulze, Anne-Katrin; Wünsch, Carsten (2002): Unterhaltung durch das Fernsehen, Eine molare Theorie, Konstanz: UVK Verlagsgesellschaft.

Gehrau, Volker (2013): Beobachtung, in: Schweiger, Wolfgang; Fahr, Andreas (Hrsg.), Handbuch Medienwirkungsforschung, Wiesbaden: Springer Fachmedien.

Gerrig, Richard. J. (1993): Experiencing Narrative Worlds, On the Psychological Activities of Reading, New Haven: Westview Press, URL: https://sites.ualberta.ca/~dmiall/LiteraryReading/Readings/Gerrig%20Experiencing%20Narrative.pdf, Abruf am 31.10.2019.

Green, M. C., & Brock, T. C. (2000): The Role of Transportation in Persuasiveness of Public Narratives. Journal of Personality and Social Psychology 79, S. 701–721, URL: http://www.communicationcache.com/uploads/1/0/8/8/10887248/the_role_of_transportation_in_the_persuasiveness_of_public_narratives.pdf, Abruf 31.10.2019.

Green, M. C., Brock, T. C., & Kaufman, G. F. (2004): Understanding Media Enjoyment: The Role of Transportation into Narrative Worlds. *Communication Theory 14*, S. 311–327.

Grodal, Torben (1999): Emotions, cognitions and narrative patterns in film, in: Platinga, Carl; Smith Greg M. (Hrsg.): Passionate views, Film, cognition and emotion, Baltimore, London: The Johns Hopkins University Press, S. 127–145.

Grots, Alexander; Pratschke, Margarete (2009): Design Thinking – Kreativität als Methode, in: Marketing Review St. Gallen 2-2009, S. 18–23. URL: https://link.springer.com/article/10.1007/s11621-009-0027-4, Abruf am 31.10.2019.

Grutzmer, Alexander (2015): Architektur und Kommunikation – Zur Medialität gebauter Wirklichkeit. Bielefeldt: Transcript Verlag.

Hartmann, Tilo; Böcking, Saskia Schramm, Holger; Wirth, Werner; Klimmt, Christoph; Vorderer, Peter (2005): Räumliche Präsenz als Rezeptionsmodalität. Ein theoretisches Modell zur Entstehung von Präsenzerleben. URL: https://www.researchgate.net/profile/Holger_Schramm/publication/257158657_Raumliche_Prasenz_als_Rezeptionsmodalitat_Ein_theoretisches_Modell_zur_Entstehung_von_Prasenzerleben/links/581e01d308aeccc08af05e06.pdf, Abruf am 12.01.2020.

Hasebrink, Uwe (2003): Nutzungsforschung, in: Bentele, Günter; Brosius, Hans-Bernd; Jarren, Otfried (Hrsg.): Öffentliche Kommunikation. Handbuch Kommunikations- und Medienwissenschaft, Wiesbaden: Westdeutscher Verlag.

Herlyn, Ulfert/Seggern, Hille von/Heinzelmann, Claudia/Karow, Daniela (2003): Jugendliche in öffentlichen Räumen der Stadt. Chancen und Restriktionen der Raumaneignung. Opladen: Leske und Budrich. S. 15–45, 112–143, 218–246.

Hickethier, Knut (2012): Film und Fernsehanalyse, 5. Aufl., Stuttgart: J.B. Metzler Verlag.

Hofer, Matthias (2013): Präsenzerleben und Teleportation, in: Schweiger, Wolfgang; Fahr, Andreas (Hrsg.): Handbuch Medienwirkungsforschung, Wiesbaden: Springer Fachmedien, S. 279–294, URL: https://www.researchgate.net/publication/258332391_Prasenzerleben_und_Transportation, Abruf am 31.10.2019.

Kahneman, Daniel (2011): Schnelles Denken, Langsames Denken, München: Siedler Verlag.

Katz, Elihu; Gurevitch, Michael; Haas, Hadassah (1973): On the Use of the Mass Media for Important Things, American Sociological Review, 38 (2), S. 164–181, URL: http://repository.upenn.edu/asc_papers/267, Abruf am 31.10.2019.

Lackes, Richard; Siepermann, Markus (2017): Stichwort: Benutzer, Gabler Wirtschaftslexikon (Hrsg.), Springer Gabler Verlag, URL: http://wirtschaftslexikon.gabler.de/Archiv/74931/benutzer-v9.html, Abruf am 31.10.2019.

Lash, S. (2002): Critique of Information, London: Sage.

Messinger, Heinz et al. (1997): Langenscheidts Großes Schulwörterbuch Englisch-Deutsch, 13. Aufl., Berlin: Langenscheidt.

Platinga, Carl (2009): Moving viewers. American film and the spectators experience, Berkeley: University of California Press.

Reinicke, Leonard (08.07.2016): Mood Management Theory, The International Encyclopedia of Media Effects, John Wiley and Sons, URL: https://www.researchgate.net/publication/319265020_Mood_Management_Theory, Download: DOI: https://doi.org/10.1002/9781118783764.wbieme0085, Abruf 31.10.2019.

Sadowski, W., & Stanney, K. (2002). Presence in virtual environments. In K. M. Stanney (Hrsg.), *Human factors and ergonomics. Handbook of virtual environments: Design, implementation, and applications* (S. 791–806). Mahwah, NJ, US: Lawrence Erlbaum Associates Publishers.

Schuemie, Martjin J.; van der Straaten, Peter.; Krijn, Merel; van der Mast, Charles. A.P.G. (2001): Research on presence in virtual reality: A survey, in: Cyber Psychology & Behavior, 4 (2), S. 183–201, URL: https://pdfs.semanticscholar.org/636f/d665abf14588929014eb28f0219fe1be75d4.pdf Abruf am 31.10.2019.

Schweiger, Wolfgang; Fahr, Andreas (2013): Vorwort, in: Schweiger, Wolfgang; Fahr, Andreas (Hrsg.): Handbuch Medienwirkungsforschung, Wiesbaden: Springer Fachmedien.

Stangl, Werner (2017): Bedürfnis, Lexikon für Psychologie und Pädagogik, URL: http://lexikon.stangl.eu/13476/beduerfnis/, Abgerufen am 31.10.2019.

Thesmann, Stefan (2016): Interface Design- Usability, Use Experience und Accessibility im Web gestalten, 2. Aufl., Wiesbaden: Springer Vieweg.

Trepte, Sabine (2013): Psychologie als Grundlage der Medienwirkungsforschung, in: Schweiger, Wolfgang; Fahr, Andreas (Hrsg.): Handbuch Medienwirkungsforschung, Wiesbaden: Springer Fachmedien, S. 89–112.

Uhrig, Meike (2015): Darstellung, Rezeption und Wirkung von Emotionen im Film – eine interdisziplinäre Studie, Wiesbaden: Springer Fachmedien.

Usoh, Martin; Arthur, Kevin; Whitton, Mary C.; Bastos, Rui (1999): Walking - Walking in Place - Flying, in Virtual Environments. Proc SIGGRAPH 1999, S. 359–364, http://citeseerx.ist.psu.edu/viewdoc/download?doi=10.1.1.33.2837&rep=rep1&type=pdf, Abruf 12.01.2020.

Witmer, Bob. G.; Singer, Michael. J. (1998): Measuring Presence in Virtual Environments: A Presence; Questionnaire. Presence: Teleoperators and Virtual Environments 7, S. 225–240, URL: https://nil.cs.uno.edu/publications/papers/witmer1998measuring.pdf, Abruf am 23.07.2017.

Wirth, Werner (2013): Grundlagen emotionaler Medienwirkungen, in: Schweiger, Wolfgang; Fahr, Andreas (Hrsg.): Handbuch der Medienwirkungsforschung, Wiesbaden: Springer Verlag, S. 227–246.

Wünsch, Carsten (2006): Unterhaltungserleben – Ein hierarchisches Zwei-Ebenen-Modell affektiv-kognitiver Informationsverarbeitung, Band 3, Köln: Herbert von Harlem Verlag.

Producers for Expert Interviews

Those who decide to work on XR projects become media makers and have to acquire new skills.

Media are subject to evolutionary changes which, as a creative process, are in a reciprocal relationship between society, the user and the actors. These influence each other (cf. Dogruel 2013, p. 318 f.). As described in Sect. 4.1, AR and VR media will fundamentally change the way people communicate and how they perceive reality. These processes of change are also reflected at the product level. The challenge for producers is to develop application possibilities that can economically benefit from this change by fulfilling user needs. As media innovations, AR and VR present producers with the particular challenge of taking these aspects into account in the production and marketing of their applications (cf. Sects. 4.3.2 and 4.4.1).

This chapter introduces the producers who were selected as experts for this scientific study. For this purpose, the term producer is defined and the initial situation of media producers is clarified. The next step is to introduce the producers and their projects, who will be interviewed as experts. For this purpose producer-specific **categories** are added to the three identified categories of **content, user and economy** of the secondary analysis in Chapters 3 to 5 as these can provide clues to success factors in the production process. These five categories form the final basis for the expert interviews and their analysis in Chap. 7.

E. Langer, *Media Innovations AR and VR*,
https://doi.org/10.1007/978-3-662-66280-9_6

6.1   Initial Situation of the Producers

The producer is generally a manufacturer and producer of a product (cf. Scholze-Stubenrecht et al. 2006, p. 809). In the economic context producer refers to an owner of a business or the primary production of the industry (cf. Voigt 2017), which can be a company or an individual. For this thesis, producer means a company that produces media content for AR and VR.

The production of media content lies within the remit of media producers, who are once again divided into film and television producers. They produce audiovisual media products that are intended to satisfy the need for entertainment and information (cf. Dreiskämper 2003, p. 21). These producers are located in the media industry.[1] The media industry is a system consisting of organizations and actors, such as publishers and television stations on the side of content distributors and media producers as producers of media content. Together with other sectors such as advertising agencies, software and games producers, the media industry is one of the 11 sub-markets of the cultural and creative industries (cf. Bertschek et al. 2016, p. 3) "Cultural and creative industries include those cultural and creative enterprises which [...] are engaged in the creation, production, distribution and/or medial dissemination of cultural/creative goods and services. The essential criterion of the definition is the commercial character of the enterprises" (Bertschek et al. 2016, p. 2).

The unifying element of all creative professionals is the creative act of creating works, content and products. Media producers are therefore creators of cultural assets with economic interests. All organizations and actors active in the media system produce media content according to market principles, such as newspapers, television and radio formats, web series and other products (cf. Jarren et al. 2013, p. 32). Media contents are economic goods with the characteristic task of satisfying needs that are produced on demand (cf. Deuerling 2015, p. 29; Kiefer 2001, p. 142). The creation of novel products is therefore inherent in the media system and forms the competence of the media producer (cf. Hickethier 2012, p. 214). As a creative entrepreneur, the latter acts on behalf of media organizations such as TV broadcasters and has the task of permanently producing novel media goods for information and entertainment purposes (cf. Deuerling 2015, p. 27; Kiefer 2001, p. 176). For this purpose media producers have an army of creative service providers at their disposal, such as authors, designers or editors, who make their creativity available as a personal property. This creativity is of existential importance for the producer (cf. Deuerling 2015, pp. 27, 77, Mueller-Oerlinghausen and Sauder 2003, pp. 22 f.). The entire organizational structure and supplier environment of the media producer are geared towards the production of creative economic goods that are intended to give their clients

---

[1] The media industry is viewed either from the perspective of economics or communication studies (cf. Fröhlich 2010, p. 35; Altmeppen and Karmasin 2003, p. 24). The latter divides it according to Luhmann's systems theory model into groups of actors, individuals and organizations at micro, meso and macro levels (cf. Seufert 2013b, p. 11 f.).

the attention of the audience. The initial economic situation is that media products are underfunded on an industry-specific basis (cf. Przybylski 2011, p. 213).

TV stations as clients set the costs and convey the creative content to an audience (cf. Jarren et al. 2013, p. 32). TV stations have a gatekeeper function. The term gatekeeper corresponds to their mass media organization through which they have direct contact with the audience. In this function, broadcasters take on a pre-selection of content (cf. Fröhlich 2010, p. 59 f.). A direct link between the media producer and the audience is not yet present in this media system. The media organization is at the centre of this media system. Since media organizations and their producers produce cultural goods and journalistic works, they bear social responsibility and are subject to state controls. In addition, factors such as audience demand and viewing habits influence the content in the media market (cf. Jarren et al. 2013, p. 33; Fröhlich 2010, p. 69). Since media producers have no access to the audience, they are dependent on external conditions. At the same time TV broadcasters are their competitors as broadcasters are urged to generate according to economic framework conditions in order to remain functional and competitive. This holds also true for fee-financed public broadcasters (cf. Deuerling 2015, p. 26; WDR December 6, 2016, p. 42).

6.1.1 Market Change Due to Media Change

The development of new technologies is changing the media system through new forms of media use, fragmentation of provider and user markets, and the diversity of media content (cf. Seufert 2013a, p. 115). Direct access to the recipient is possible via smartphones and computers, which facilitates access to the media system for new actors (cf. Przybylski 2011, p. 216). Companies appear as producers and distributors that are not part of the cultural and creative industries. These are, for example, travel companies such as TUI, which is building a branded-content platform around the topic of travel. The content comes from a total of 600 channels of the sub-companies' social networks (cf. Pfannenmüller 2017). Google launches entertainment shows on its YouTube video channel, for which the Internet entrepreneur acquires the advertising partners itself (cf. App 2017).

AR and VR are new media that convey novel content for information, knowledge and entertainment purposes via data glasses and smartphones. In order to use the new hardware devices, a variety of offers for different types of use are needed that are tailored to the AR and VR media and create spatial experiences. The travel company TUI provides its customers with VR glasses for a 360° exploration of holiday destinations for marketing purposes (cf. Mühl 2017). On the other hand, car manufacturers, museums, architects, as well as the travel and advertising industry develop content for VR and AR (cf. Heim and Dertinger 2017). Accordingly, hardware manufacturers and platform operators such as Facebook, Snapchat, Instagram and Google are pursuing the strategy of focusing on user-generated experiences and are providing corresponding tools (cf. Sect. 1.1). The community platforms Snapchat, TikTok and Instagram provide users with AR tools with which they can embellish themselves or their surroundings with fun 2D and 3D objects.

Professional software for developers, game designers, and other creatives include programs such as Unreal or Unity, ARKit/ARCore, Tilt Brush Sketches, or content management systems (CMS) such as those from Blippar, Shoutr Labs, or Adobe that allow professionals to produce high-quality experiences for VR and AR applications (see Google Poly 2019; Blippar 2019; Shoutr Labs 2019).

At the same time home furnishing companies like IKEA are developing their own AR apps to support their sales. Customers can use the AR app IKEA Place to furnish their home with virtual furniture in advance (cf. IKEA 2018).

As explained in Sect. 6.1, the core business and core competence of media producers lies in the creation of new audiovisual products that fulfil a user need. Space and the physical presence of a user in the medium are the media-specific characteristics of AR and VR identified in Sect. 4.2.3 (cf. Section 4.2.3).

Producers are now faced with the challenge of developing products that take into account the physical experience of the user and the space, while at the same time fulfilling a user need. Media producers from the creative industries share this starting position with VR and AR producers from the industry. For all of them producing AR and VR experiences means, on the one hand, establishing new production areas within the company. On the other hand, the producers are faced with the task of identifying new user needs that can only be satisfied through the media use of AR and VR (cf. Section 4.4 and Chap. 5).

The analysis of success factors in Chap. 7 will show which minimum requirements should be guaranteed on the production and user level in order to successfully produce AR and VR products.

6.1.2   Summary

Section 6.1 made it clear that the change in the media and the associated economic conditions are changing the starting position of media producers. The term media producer can be extended to include companies that also produce media products and are not active in the media industry or the cultural and creative industries. This also applies to the production of AR and VR applications as production is cross-sectoral (cf. Section 1.1). Since, in addition to competence, the initial situation, motivation and insights are also relevant for the production of AR and VR applications, these aspects form category 4 (producer) and category 5 (learnings). The term media producer will be standardized in the following by the term producer.

6.2   Expert Interviews

The survey of different AR and VR producers intends to give information about production-related approaches and content-related factors that can contribute to the production of AR amd VR applications that provide users with a media-specific experience. This is based on the assumption that media use is the need for entertainment, excitement and information and that the experience of presence and transportation are media-specific characteristics (cf. Section 5.3). The factors that satisfy a user need and promote a positive media experience are determined in the expert interview.

6.2.1   Categories for the Expert Interviews

The expert interviews are based on the five categories developed in the secondary analysis in Chapters 3 to 6. These are divided into the producer level and the user level. At the user level are categories 1 (content) and 2 (user experience), which look at content factors and the consideration of user needs. Both categories are examined for cues that contribute to creating a media-specific experience for the user.

   The producer level in categories 3 (economy) and 4 (producer) identifies which knowledge of innovation development and specific framework conditions favor the production of user-related AR and VR applications. Category 5 (learnings) considers both levels (cf. Table 6.1). Subcategories were formed for the interview guide and specific aspects were queried (cf. Appendix 5 Interview guide).

6.3   The AR and VR Producer Experts

In the following, the nine producers, who are interviewed in the expert interview and describe their AR and VR productions will be presented. The presentation integrates aspects of the producer level of categories 3 (economy) and 4 (producer), such as the initial situation and motivation. For the description of the projects, content aspects are added for better understanding, such as story, spatial representation and interaction. The selected producers produce AR and VR applications for entertainment purposes and knowledge transfer. Among them there are three AR and five VR applications and one MR project in a CAVE. The compilation of producers forms a focus group that is assumed to have skills and experience to produce AR and VR projects. The diversity of perspectives forms the quality of the expert interviews: It is further assumed that the more diverse the views on user needs, approaches and experiences are, the more knowledge can be gained from the interviews and the broader is the spectrum of potential success factors.

   All producers are named and given codes for ease of analysis, which can be followed in the analysis steps and in the original transcripts (see Appendix 1–4). The approach to

Table 6.1 Overview of categories for expert interviews

Categories	Subcategories	Aspects
Content User level	Media format	Technology Purpose approach
	Stories and content	Form of dramaturgy Three-dimensionality content Special features of the content
	Space and interaction	Three-dimensionality space Representation of media integration Interaction space, three-dimensionality
	Approach user needs	Consideration of user needs, media use and target group
Users User level	User reactions Media usage	Experience, reactions General
	User experience Entertainment and information	Motivation for entertainment, information, communication
	Interaction and communication experience	Application as a group, alone with objects
	Space and body experience	Three-dimensional spatial perception Movement, presence experience Body experience Sensory stimuli
	Experience with avatars/ Actors/protagonists	Communication and interaction with protagonists/actors/colleagues
Economics Producer level	Team	Competence External competence and partners
	Production	Costs, time Approach, management Financial framework
	Market potential	Added value for companies Identifiable user needs Business models and clients
	Ecosystem	Partner, exchange, Cooperation, collaboration
Producer Producer level	Initial situation and motivation	Previous experience In-house development, research project Task/objective Market leadership
Learnings Producer and user level	Personal insights Advantages AR and VR Assessment according to strengths and weaknesses Other	Assessments according to important findings in the previous categories and personal insights

Source: Own representation

the analysis is explained in Appendix 7. An overview of all files of the analysis can be found in Appendix 6.

6.3.1   West German Broadcasting Corporation

WDR (Westdeutscher Rundfunk[2]) is producing its first VR project in 2017, entitled "Dom360 –Der Kölner Dom – wie ihr ihn noch nicht erlebt habt". The novel project is located in the Internet program area of the Innovation Lab department. The aim is to build up the development of new skills for virtual and augmented reality at the station. The team consists of four editors and one writer, including the project manager, science editor Thomas Hallet.[3] Technical service providers for camera and app development will be brought in from outside on a selective basis. The project is funded as an innovation project with a budget in the amount of a high-quality documentary (author's note: approx. 250,000–350,000 EUR). The project duration was around 9 months.

To date, WDR has implemented further VR and AR projects as well as 360° videos and has received several awards for some productions. Among them are the two projects "Glückauf" and "Zeitkapsel" (cf. Figures 6.1 and 6.2).

Fig. 6.1 Screenshot WDR VR project "Glückauf", 2018 (Source: WDR [own representation])

---

[2] The public broadcaster produces and distributes media content with the mandate to offer all citizens in the broadcast area free access to information, education, culture and entertainment. The programming mandate is derived from the Grundgesetz, Article 5(2), and is enshrined in the broadcasting treaty. The WDR-Gesetz § 4 defines the programming mandate of WDR (cf. WDR December 6, 2016, p. 7).

[3] The persons are named in the introduction. In the analysis they are given codes. The codes can be traced on the basis of the overview of the experts (cf. Appendix 1).

Fig. 6.2 Screenshot WebVR – project "Zeitkapsel": "Welcome on Board 1960" (Source: WDR)

Both projects were realized for the first time as a WebVR application. This means that they are browser-based and the user can experience the 360° worlds on a computer monitor without VR glasses (cf. WDR 2018a, b).

With the AR project WDR "AR 1933–1945", the public broadcaster brings wartime witnesses via smartphone and tablet to the users, wherever they are (see WDR March 29, 2019).

The expert interview and the following analysis are based on the first VR project of WDR. For this purpose, WDR is referred to as the producer (1B1).

6.3.1.1 VR Project DOM360.Wdr.de

The goal is to "work out something that should really be a special experience in the immersive perception of the user [...] we first only had the idea of how it could work but no tools" (1B1). Five established media formats are used in the VR application, such as 2D videos, computer-generated interactive environment, 360° videos, 360° and 2D photos, sound and text (cf. WDR 2019a). The user is alone in the application. He stands in a VR 360° photo visualization in the choir area of the Cologne Cathedral, a place that is normally inaccessible to the visitor (cf. WDR 2019b). The sign systems anchored in the space are, on the one hand, the symbols anchored in the cathedral such as crucifixes, icons and altars and, on the other hand, the representations integrated in the virtual space. These point to further media formats such as 360° videos, photos or text information. "Interactions", so-called "hotspots", were built in, which lead to navigation in the room and to the contents. The user is offered six different types of content, such as a discovery with the title, "mysterious corners" and a "journey through time" (cf. WDR 2019c). The criterion for narrative variants for the user's entertainment experience was: "What could our users presumably be most interested in?" (1B1). The stories most appealing to the team were discussed among them using brainstorming and associations and then sorted by how effective they were.

Fig. 6.3 Screenshot WDR website Dom360 "Mysterious Places", 2017 (Source: WDR)

The user's interaction in the experience is rewarded "but the reward always has to be that I get to discover a new thought, a new impression, a new piece of information then just for me" (1B1). For time travel, real actors are placed in a CGI environment to tell their story at the location. In the process the user jumps to different times through interactions. The use of binaural[4] sound enables a 360° sound experience via headphones (cf. Figure 6.3).

The sound is based on the user's line of sight and position, for example flying through the choir area of the cathedral while the choir sings below the user (cf. Dom360 2019d). The challenges lay in the complexity of the whole project. The approach was exploratory and on call as everyone sat separately. All ideas were developed, discussed, discarded and decided together as a team, starting with the development of the content and ending with the integration of user-relevant content.

The WDR project Dom360 was awarded the Grimme Online Award 2017 (see WDR June 30, 2017).

6.3.2 UFA Lab and UFA Serial Drama

The production companies UFA Lab (today merged into UFA X) and UFA Serial Drama[5] are two independent production companies of the UFA Group with different tasks (cf. UFA 2019). UFA Lab produces movies and products primarily for digital media. UFA

---

[4] Binaural sound is the spatial representation of sound that can be used for dramaturgical purposes through acoustic distance simulations. This enhances the user's feeling of being present in the room (cf. Bible 2016).

[5] The UFA Group is part of the Bertelsmann Group. The media group operates internationally with other companies and groups. In Germany, in addition to book, music and magazine publishers such as Gruner & Jahr, the RTL broadcasting group and advertising agencies belong to it (see Bertelsmann 2019). UFA Lab was transformed into UFA X as a new company. Since the interviews were conducted in 2017, UFA Lab is the producer in this book.

Serial Drama produces fictional feature movies and series for television. In collaboration with the Fraunhofer Heinrich Hertz Institut, UFA Lab and UFA Serial Drama, the project "Gateway to Infinity[6]" was developed and implemented as a technical and content prototype. In the 90-second VR application, the Fraunhofer technology 3D-Human-Body-Reconstruction (3D-HBR) is to be tested in a feasibility study. The UFA companies pursued the goal of using their storytelling expertise to further develop the film alphabet and to test how emotions can be aroused in the user in the new medium. In addition, a production workflow and a new business field for VR will be developed in the company.

This prototype for volumetric studio productions with the 3D HBR system is the cornerstone for the foundation of the Volumetric Studio in Babelsberg in 2017 (see Sect. 3.3.3).

The team consisted of three creatives from UFA Lab, technical experts and visual artists from UFA Serial Drama and the research team from the Fraunhofer Institut. The budget is estimated to be in the order of a commercial film budget, which is around one million euros.

In the analysis, UFA Lab is referred to as Producer 2 and UFA Serial Drama as Producer 3. In the expert interview, Floris Asche (2B1) and Daniel Brückner (2B2) from UFA Lab are available for content-related questions. For visual and technical-strategic aspects Frank Govaere (3B1) and Ernst Feiler (3B2) from UFA Serial Drama were interviewed.

6.3.2.1 Gateway to Infinity VR Project

The Gateway to Infinity VR project is a 180° CGI prototype application with integration of real people into a virtual environment. The short fictional scene takes place on an alien planet. The user stands on a high grid platform and observes the dialogue of a man and a woman guarding the gateway to infinity. Alongside, a spaceship flies around. The user can look around at a 360° angle and get close to the people. However, they do not perceive him. There are no interaction possibilities. The project was produced in a greenbox studio in which the actors were filmed with 32 cameras from an angle of 180° (cf. Section 3.3.3). The video of the making of "Gateway to Infinity" can be viewed on YouTube (cf. Fraunhofer 2017).

The concept was developed by the author Floris Asche, pitched to the team and broadly visualized as a process in several detailed sketches. The team is familiar with the use of such methods as well as design thinking to develop narrative and user scenarios.

The science fiction genre matched the CGI presentation and borrows ideas from Star Wars. The dialogue of the actors quickly introduces the story. The idea was that a story is directed and the user's view is guided through cinematic means. This is done "either quite directly through the speech in the picture [or] eyes looking at me, which is always a means that focuses me, [...] [or] an explosion, then I have to look there because all of a sudden the lighting conditions change" (2B1).

---

[6]The press release of UFA and UFA Lab as well as the video of the production "Gateway to Infinity" contain more details about the project (cf. UFA X 2019; Fraunhofer 2017).

6.3.3 Miriquidi Film

The film producer Miriquidi Film has small creative offices in Munich, Leipzig, Potsdam and Los Angeles (see Miriquidi Film 2018). Its core business is film and television productions, transmedia projects, gaming and 3D VR films. The unique selling point of the production company is innovative projects that are a novelty for the company and the media industry. Serial productions are not produced. The focus is on content-related media innovations and associated software programming. The AR project presented in this paper was produced in co-production with Paste-Up and funded by the state. The Hochschule Anhalt, Department of Design, was involved. Michael Geidel, managing director of Miriquidi Film, took over the coordination and development of the interactive elements of the overall project, including an AR application including app, which is a novelty for the company and for which a dedicated AR system was programmed.

In the analysis Miriquidi Film 4 and Michael Geidel are named (4B1).

6.3.3.1 Project AR-App Pastors' Children

The AR project was produced as part of a travelling exhibition on the occasion of the Luther Year 2017. The main medium is a documentary film on the topic of pastors' children and the installation of the exhibition. Additionally, a web documentation and an AR app were produced as interactive elements (cf. Geidel and Zumpe 2016). Since the installation had a spatial limitation, VR or AR applications were up for discussion. The decision was made in favor of the AR application as it was cheaper to produce and digitally extended the limited installation space. The AR application was developed by Miriquidi Film in terms of content and technology. It supplements the exhibition with additional interactive elements, such as film clips and additional information, which the user can view via the AR app in his smartphone (Fig. 6.4).

6.3.4 Exit VR

EXIT VR is a Berlin-based VR start-up that developed the walk-through location-based VR game "Huxley" and opened it in 2017 (cf. Huxley 2017). It is a holodeck for a virtual escape room game[7] that is played as a VR adventure. The motivation is also the business model of the project: to give people the opportunity to play with the technology and software by buying a ticket. Co-founder is Sven Häberlein, who has a film background as a cinematographer. At hackathons, Häberlein and his colleague discovered the potential "that there is more to it" (5B1).

---

[7] Escape rooms are games in which groups have to try to escape from a room within a time frame. In doing so, they have to solve puzzles (cf. Stückler 2015; Exit VR 2017).

Fig. 6.4 AR application for exhibition "Pastors' Children" for "Luther Year 2017" (Source: Michael Geidel)

The team consists of programmers, escape room game experts, concept and visual designers as well as VR film and game experts. At the time of the survey, the start-up is financed exclusively from its own funds. In the analysis EXIT VR is producer 5, Sven Häberlein is marked with (5B1).

6.3.4.1 VR Project Huxley

The game is a walk-through virtual space that becomes visible via the VR glasses. It represents a mixture of a power plant and a cathedral, reminiscent of the setting of the movie Metropolis. The story is set in 3007 in a space station where players must prevent an apocalypse by solving difficult and easy puzzles. It is meant to appeal to the masses (Fig. 6.5).

The players book a holodeck for the game duration of 50 minutes as a group, in which they play together. The game was created in two workshops through an exploratory approach with the experience of creative techniques to develop the story and gameplay. The skills and ideas of the participants were used in a kind of Writers Room.[8] The starting point was oneself as a user or player. "We always said you have this opportunity now, [...] you can fly, you can do magic, you can do whatever you want." (5B1).

---

[8] A Writers Room is a creative workshop in which several writers and other participants use creative methods such as design thinking and user experience design to develop stories for film and theatre, among other things (cf. Bayerisches Filmzentrum 2019).

Fig. 6.5 EXIT VR Adventure Game "Huxley1" (Source: EXIT Adventure GmbH)

The basis for deciding on the room design was the viability of the setting and its authenticity. "If you create a digital space, it's very difficult to make that space come across realistically and not like a computer game." (5B1). The limitation of space is played around with dramaturgical means.

Special offers are made to the user "so that he forgets that there are of course things that do not work" (5B1).

Interaction and navigation in the game are done via controllers. Players communicate with each other in real time via headphones and microphones. Sensory elements such as a vibrating plate complement the VR experiences.

6.3.5 Illusion Walk

In 2015, the start-up Illusion Walk from Bergisch Gladbach developed a walk-through holodeck called Immersive Deck (cf. Illusion Walk 2019). It was initially developed as a game, discarded and later further developed as an application example for training purposes for extraordinary places. The two founders Jim and Julien Rüggeberg are career changers in the media industry. Jim Rüggeberg previously worked in the tooling industry, but his interest has been in VR for 25 years. Julien Rüggeberg studied medical informatics and then game design and development. Both founders bring business and programming skills to the table. The team was complemented by further game experts. The financing of the technical and content production of the deck comes from their own funds. In addition, there will be smaller research projects. The budgets are not known.

In the paper Illusion Walk is referred to as Producer 6. Managing director Jim Rüggeberg (6B2) and the head of scientific projects, Andrea Heuck (6B1), are interviewed in the expert interview.

6.3.5.1 VR Project Immersive Deck

The holodeck is installed in a 150 square meter room. In the training application, the user enters a gate and then enters the virtual representation of a wind turbine platform in the middle of the sea (cf. Illusion Walk KG December 20, 2016). The user experiences the whole process in a walk-through application in the form of a dramaturgical tour. There he experiences "the right experience [...] and knows how to move, what to do" (6B1) as spatial visualizations such as doors and elevators give the user the feeling that he can move freely through several rooms and levels, although he is in a limited space. From the lower platform to the upper level, the user travels up an elevator, which is actually a vibrating plate that simulates the elevator experience. Furthermore, the training simulation uses virtual touch displays and additional haptic elements that the user controls with his hands. The users experience themselves as half avatars with hands and upper body. They see the other users in the virtual space as legless avatars. They can talk to them via headsets and microphones (Fig. 6.6).

Fig. 6.6 Example image from video Immersive Deck by Illusion Walk (Source: Illusion Walk Jim Rüggeberg)

The approach to the project is based on knowledge of economic innovation development. "We haven't done anything with film before, nor have we done anything with media in the form. [...] We keep running into this issue in production [...] that my staff is too gaming-heavy, not enough film. Somewhere in between [lies] [...] the approach [...] these other types of production [in film, television, computer games] give you a guideline and in the end [...] a production method [...] or a guideline [comes out]." (6B2).

For this purpose, the team derived methods from scripts and film production processes and follows game mechanisms. Product development is carried out according to business aspects. "How much added value do I generate in terms of the viewer, i.e. the customer? Because that's what ultimately counts in the marketplace." (6B2).

After 3 years of experience in implementing VR experiences, through studies, market analysis, over 200 testers and a repositioning, Illusion Walk understands the holodeck as a content provider. "We want to give people the good feeling of having gone through an adventure together." (6B1).

6.3.6   Konzerthaus Berlin

Since 2016, the Konzerthaus Berlin has been developing innovative mediation concepts for classical music in digital space as part of a multi-year research project together with the Information and Communication Applications (INKA) research group at the Hochschule für Technik und Wirtschaft (HTW) Berlin (cf. Konzerthaus Berlin 2019a). Within the framework of the EU-funded project "Apollo", several VR, 360° video, and augmented reality projects are being developed, whose goal is the innovative mediation of classical music in digital space. The AR app Konzerthaus Plus is being developed for the augmented reality projects (cf. Thoma, Annette April 5, 2017).

The project leaders on the Konzerthaus Berlin side are Albrecht Sensch,[9] who contributes his technical knowledge, and musicologist Annette Thoma. The team of two discusses each step in close collaboration with the Konzerthaus Berlin and the developers and programmers at HTW Berlin, giving equal consideration to the content and technical perspectives for the development.

The implementation of the VR and AR projects of the Konzerthaus Berlin, such as the user guidance of the AR app, was carried out by students and research assistants of the research group Information and Communication Applications (scientific director of the research group: Prof. Dr. Dr. h.c. mult. Jürgen Sieck) of the Hochschule für Technik und Wirtschaft Berlin.

This work focuses on the first AR project, the AR app Konzerthaus Plus with the 2017/2018 season brochure.

Albrecht Sensch (7B1) and Annette Thoma (7B2) are participants in the expert interview.

---

[9] Albrecht Sensch is no longer with the team as of July 2019.

6.3.6.1 AR Project AR App Konzerthaus Plus

The Konzerthaus Berlin's first AR application for the AR app Konzerthaus Plus is a combination of the 2017/2018 season brochure and linked digital content made visible via the app.

The season brochure 2017/2018[10] is offered as a print edition and in digital form for download. The digital information contained in the brochure is common media such as photos, videos, graphics and texts. Similar AR applications are also offered in the 2018/2019 season brochure (cf. Konzerthaus Berlin 2019b).

The hidden virtual content is referred to in the brochure by a mobile phone symbol, so that the brochure remains an independent medium. The additional digital content only becomes visible with the AR app (Fig. 6.7).

The AR app is connected to the smartphone camera. By opening the app, the camera is automatically activated and makes the digital content, such as images, videos, texts and sounds, visible in the brochure. In this way the media space of the brochure is expanded

Fig. 6.7 Extract from the season brochure 2017/2018 Konzerthaus Berlin (Source: Konzerthaus Berlin)

---

[10] The 2017/2018 season brochure is no longer available for download.

Fig. 6.8 Screenshot AR app with season brochure 2017/2018 Konzerthaus Berlin (Source: Konzerthaus Berlin)

by virtual offers. Applications include, for example, a 3D representation of the concert hall, which appears on the smartphone display; the user can view it from all sides. At the same time a musical sequence is played (Fig. 6.8).

The digital extension of the medium also works for the digital output on the monitor. The app visualizes a 3D representation of the Konzerthaus that protrudes from the monitor. The 3D model of the Konzerthaus was expanded and refined for the 2018/2019 season brochure, for example with exterior textures, five halls and interaction options. The user recognizes the videos by the triangular start symbol, which is known for starting videos or audio files.

A few pages further on, the AR user embarks on a musical journey through the Baltic States. A map of the Baltic countries is visualized in the brochure. The AR app expands the map with graphic animations that open up when the smartphone is moved over them. Music excerpts are played for each country, which become dynamically louder when the smartphone is moved closer. This happens because the camera in the smartphone scans the markers hidden in the image and automatically plays the information hidden in them. The AR offer in the app is constantly being expanded (cf. Thoma, Annette June 26, 2017).

Another AR project is the Virtual Quartet, in which musicians play the beginning of the string quartet "Death and the Maiden" ("Der Tod und das Mädchen") by Franz Schubert virtually on a sheet of A4 cards (Fig. 6.9). The special feature of this project, developed in 2018, is that the musicians and their instruments can be heard individually. For this purpose each musician is assigned a playing card. If a playing card is removed from the camera's field of vision, not only the musician on it disappears, but also his or her individual

Fig. 6.9 Konzerthaus Berlin "Virtual Quartet" (Source: Konzerthaus Berlin)

voice – thus a string quartet quickly becomes a duo or even a solo. For this purpose the musicians were recorded individually in a green-screen studio and in the anechoic room of the Technischen Universität Berlin. The 2D video created for each artist was linked to their map using image markers. Via the AR app Konzerthaus Plus, the virtual musicians become visible on the maps and audible as a quartet[11] (cf. Thoma, Annette June 4, 2018).

The AR app can be used with the season brochure, in the exhibition at the Konzerthaus, at home and in schools. It thus offers a high added value for innovative music education.

6.3.7 Cologne Games Lab

The Cologne Games Lab is part of the Technischen Hochschule Köln and sees itself as a provider of impulses to the economy for the development of new types of games, which are used, among other things, to impart knowledge. The institute develops and researches new forms of inactive knowledge transfer through game approaches and 3D visualizations and develops showcases for the economy.

---

[11] A detailed project description can be found on the website of the Virtual Concert Hall at http:// virtuelles-konzerthaus.de/das-virtuelle-quartett/

The AR app HisToGo[12] was developed and implemented as an AR game in a three-year research project for interactive history learning. The project was led by Katharina Tillmanns from the Cologne Games Lab, in collaboration with a team from the Historisches Institut at the University of Cologne. The project was funded by the RheinEnergie Foundation. The amount of funding is not known. The follow-up project is funded with 300,000 EUR over 3 years. Research director and co-director is Prof. Dr. Björn Bartholdy. The Cologne Games Lab has already produced several AR and VR applications. For this work it is selected as a reference producer that seeks to integrate the player-centered approach of game development for the development of AR and VR applications in order to investigate the success factors. Cologne Games Lab producer 8 is named for the analysis. Experts are Dr. Björn Bartholdy (8B1) and Katharina Tillmanns (8B2).

6.3.7.1 Project AR-App HisToGo

With the AR app HisToGo, users go on a mission together in the Cologne city area to find historical artifacts at original sites and solve puzzles. The advantages of the project lie in the enhanced virtual representation of the architecture of 2000 years ago at the original locations. "So really standing in a place and rediscovering in life size at least a section of what life was like, in this case, 2000 years ago" (8B2). The engagement with details and the subject is seen as a learning effect, the engagement with the AR game is seen as immersion. Novelty is the social component as a multiplayer game and shared learning. Each player has different information. Only together they lead to the success of the missions. Curiosity is aroused because "no overall story is told, but we tell many short episodes divided into missions" (8B2). The mission is put together rather roughly to foreground learning and game mechanics. Which "sort of gives a taste of what the wholeness of this project should look like." (8B2).

HisToGo can be rated as an entertainment game because "the learning goal was not put in the foreground" (8B2). HisToGo is also fun for adults because the content offers a challenge for different levels of knowledge and also offers them the opportunity to dicover the content..

6.3.8   Rolls Royce

Rolls Royce is a British manufacturer of aircraft engines, among other things, with its headquarters in Dahlewitz in Brandenburg. The project presented here is called VITIII (Virtual Engine or Virtual Trubor Machinery, Version 3) and was implemented as part of a 3-year research project from 2011 to 2014 with the Universität Cottbus. It is still being developed. The project leader is Computational Fluid Dynamics (CFD) engineer Dr.

---

[12] The project HisToGo was completed in 2017. (Cf. Cologne Games Lab 2017).

Fig. 6.10   CAVE engine at Rolls Royce (Source: Rolls Royce)

Marius Swoboda, who works on data visualization in the fluid mechanics of aircraft engines. The visualization of complex system processes was previously carried out using digital 2D representations and PowerPoint presentations. On this basis, new developments were designed and economic decisions were made. The Mixed Reality application has simplified the process and is now an important component for the development and improvement of aircraft engines at Rolls Royce. Dr. Marius Swoboda (9B1) is available as an expert (cf. von Ammon 2016; Fig. 6.10).

Several departments are involved in the design and further development of an engine. Each develops its plans in parallel and for itself, partly around the plans of the other departments. The idea was to make the technical data of an engine visible in real time for everyone at the same time. "We just had such a jumble of data. [...] We wanted to display the content [...] vision, that was pretty much the most important thing and the need to just see stuff differently." (9B1) The basis for the decision for the project was, among other things, a scientific study by Ware and Franck (1996)[13] on 3D visualizations, according to

---

[13] Cockburn and McKenzie cite Waren and Franck's studies in the SIGCHI'01, March 31–April 4 issue (see Cockburn and McKenzie 2001, p. 2).

which people make fewer mistakes in a 3D visualization. "In 2D, out of 100 details, 40% were errors. So 40 details you don't recognize. Now when you see the same scene tracked in 3D, that error rate goes down to ten percent. That is, you just make fewer errors in 3D." (9B2).

The virtual space is created by a CAVE, consisting of three rear projection walls of 350×200 m. The user wears semi-transparent data glasses through which the virtual engine becomes visible in 3D. The virtual engine model consists of over 20,000 individual parts. It is based on real data from the designers' drawing program. "You can simply see details much better." (9B2). The gesture control was developed intuitively by the developers, without prior knowledge of user experience or psychology. The interface and gesture control were a big issue. "So as an example then this swipe on the iPhone. How do you do that in space?" (9B2). In addition to the exploratory approach to technical implementation, user behavior was also explored psychologically, "We're engineers, [that] wasn't a psychological consideration of what was worked out there, that was just a feeling, our feeling." (9B2).

The semi-transparent mixed reality glasses integrate the real physical space into the virtual simulation. This is perceived as more pleasant and natural. Communication plays an important role in construction processes. "Seeing the other people next to you, despite the glasses and despite the same immersion." (9B2). The colleague appears as a real person in the scene. "So, you are always immersive in that scene, in the 3D scene." (9B2). The same 3D perspective makes it easier to discuss problems. The departments that worked on one engine through interfaces found it difficult to discuss the complex processes and come up with solutions. "Now they're both in this CAVE and just discussing ways to make it more orderly [...] With the effect that our new designs [...] look much more orderly to outsiders as well." (9B2).

6.3.9 Summary

The presentation of the nine producers shows that the projects and the starting points of the producers are very different. On the one hand, we are dealing with AR and VR projects, each of which has different objectives. On the other hand, motivational differences in dealing with AR and VR, as well as the starting position, indicate that different economic interests are being pursued. The approach of product development also allows conclusions about knowledge of innovation developments. This aspect is examined for success factors regarding the approach to user needs. Factors relevant to production, such as team composition and methodological approaches, are also taken into account. These two factors are added as subcategories of category 3 (economy) (cf. Annex 2 Overview of categories).

Literature

Altmeppen, Klaus-Dieter; Karmasin, Matthias (2003); Medienökonomie als transdisziplinäres Lehr- und Forschungsprogramm, in: K.-D. Altmeppen & M. Karmasin (Hrsg.): Medien und Ökonomie, Band 1/1: Grundlagen der Medienökonomie, Wiesbaden: Westdeutscher Verlag, S. 19–51.

Ammon, Cornelia von (2016): Virtual Reality im Triebwerkbau wird Realität, Bundesverband Deutscher Luft- und Raumfahrt, URL: https://www.bdli.de/innovation-der-woche/virtual-reality-im-triebwerksbau-wird-realitaet, Abruf am 02.11.2019.

App, Ulrike (05.05.2017): Neue Webserien, YouTube setzt auf Promi-Faktor YouTube arbeitet an verschiedenen Promi-Shows. Google sucht dafür Werbepartner, URL: https://www.wuv.de/digital/neue_webserien_youtube_setzt_auf_promi_faktor, Abruf am 02.11.2019.

Bayerisches Filmzentrum (2019): Suchbegriff Writers Room Veröffentlichung, URL: http://filmzentrum-bayern.de/veranstaltungen/writers-roomlab/, Abruf am 02.11.2019.

Bertelsmann (2019): URL: http://www.bertelsmann.de/#st-1-, Abruf am 02.11.2019.

Bertschek, Irene, Ohnemus, Jörg et al. (2016): Bundesministerium für Wirtschaft und Energie, Monitoringbericht 2016: Ausgewählte wirtschaftliche Eckdaten der Kultur- und Kreativwirtschaft Kurzfassung, Berlin: Bundesministerium für Wirtschaft und Energie (BMWi), URL: https://www.bmwi.de/Redaktion/DE/Publikationen/Wirtschaft/kuk-monitoringbericht-2016-kurzfassung.pdf?__blob=publicationFile&v=18-, Abruf am 02.11.2019.

Bible, Thomas (31.05.2016): Binauraler Sound Oculus Story, URL: https://www.oculus.com/story-studio/blog/binaural-audio-for-narrative-vr/, Abruf am 02.11.2019.

Blippar (2019), URL: https://www.blippar.com/build-ar/augmented-reality-education, Abruf am 02.11.2019.

Cockburn, Andy & McKenzie, Bruce. (2001). 3D or not 3D? Evaluating the effect of the third dimension in a document management system. 434–441. https://doi.org/10.1145/365024.365309. URL: http://www.cosc.canterbury.ac.nz/andrew.cockburn/papers/chi01DM.pdf, Abruf am 02.11.2019.

Cologne Games Lab (2017): Research, HisToGo (2015 – 2017), URL: http://www.colognegamelab.de/research/histogo/, Abruf am 02.11.2019.

Deuerling, Tanja (2015): Innovationsmanagement für neues Fernsehen – Entwicklungen von Bewegtbildformaten in Abhängigkeit vom Innovationsgrad, Wiesbaden: Springer VS.

Dogruel, Leyla (2013): Eine Kommunikationswissenschaftliche Konzeption von Medieninnovation – Begriffsverständnisse und theoretische Zugänge, Wiesbaden: Springer Fachmedien.

Dreiskämper, Thomas (2003): Medienökonomie I: Lehrbuch für Studiengänge medienorientierter Berufe: Konzeptionsansätze und theoretische Fundierungen der Medienökonomie, Münster: Lit-Verlag.

Exit VR (19.05.2017): HUXLEY – Das erste VR Live Adventure, URL: https://www.youtube.com/watch?v=BlCA5m9gHGI, Abruf am 02.11.2019.

Fröhlich, Kerstin (2010): Innovationssysteme der TV-Unterhaltungsproduktion, Komparative Analyse Deutschlands und Großbritanniens, Wiesbaden: GWV Fachverlage GmbH.

Fraunhofer HHI (22.04.2017): Making Of „Gateway to Infinity", volumetric virtual reality experience, URL: https://www.youtube.com/watch?v=8h6i2_3xDcs, Abruf am 02.11.2019.

Geidel, Michael.; Zumpe, Angela (2016): Pfarrers Kinder – Installation, URL: http://www.pfarrerskinder.de/installation/, Abruf am 02.11.2019.

Google, Poly (2019): Tilt Brush- Skizzen (2019): URL: https://poly.google.com/tiltbrush, Abruf am 02.11.2019.

Hickethier, Knut (2012): Film und Fernsehanalyse, 5. Aufl., Stuttgart: J.B. Metzler Verlag.

Heim, Andreas, Dertinger, Heiko (15.03.2017): Deutscher Markenreport 2017, Brandoffice, Absatzwirtschaft (Hrsg.), URL: https://www.absatzwirtschaft.de/deutscher-markenreport-2017-virtual-augmented-reality-im-marketing-grosse-erwartungen-aber-wenig-know-how-101341/, Abruf am 02.11.2019.

IKEA (19.03.2018): IKEA Launces IKEA Place, a New App, That Allows People to Virtually Place Furniture in Their Home, URL: https://www.ikea.com/us/en/this-is-ikea/newsroom/ikea-place-app-launches-on-android-allowing-millions-of-people-to-reimagine-home-furnishings-pubae2b1d71; Abruf am 02.11.2019.

Illusion Walk KG (20.12.2016): Virtual Reality: Holodeck – Follow us into the Immersive, URL: https://www.youtube.com/watch?v=GxeWyuvVzeA, Abruf am 02.11.2019.

Illusion Walk KG (2019), URL: https://www.illusion-walk.com/, Abruf am 02.11.2019.

Jarren, Otfried; Studer, Samuel; Künzler, Matthias (2013): Mediensystemwandel als Medienorganisationswandel – Implikationen der Population-Ecology, in: Seufert, Wolfgang; Sattelberger, Felix (Hrsg.): Langfristiger Wandel von Medienstrukturen – Theorien, Methoden, Befunde, Baden-Baden: Nomos Verlagsgesellschaft, S. 31–50.

Kiefer, Marie Luise (2001): Medienökonomik, Einführung in eine ökonomische Theorie der Medien. München: De Gruyter Oldenbourg.

Konzerthaus Berlin (2019a): Virtuelles Konzerthaus, URL: https://www.konzerthaus.de/de/virtuelles-konzerthaus, Abruf am 02.11.2019.

Konzerthaus Berlin (2019b): Saison URL: https://www.konzerthaus.de/de/saison, Abruf am 02.11.2019.

Miriquidi Film (2018): Projekte, URL: http://www.miriquidifilm.de/projekte/?lang=de, Abruf am 02.11.2019.

Mühl, Melanie (01.05.2017): Als wären wir schon da URL: http://www.faz.net/aktuell/feuilleton/debatten/virtual-reality-bei-thomas-cook-und-tui-14991137.html, Abruf am 02.11.2019.

Mueller-Oerlinghausen, Jens; Sauder, Axel (2003): Kreativität. Alles oder nichts? Erfolgsfaktoren innovativer Produktentwicklung. in: F. Habann (Hrsg.): Innovationsmanagement in Medienunternehmen, Theoretische Grundlagen und Praxiserfahrungen, Wiesbaden: Gabler, S. 15–36.

Pfannenmüller, Judith (16.01.2017): Das plant Tui für seine Branded Content Plattform: URL:https://www.wuv.de/marketing/das_plant_tui_fuer_seine_branded_content_plattform, Abruf am 02.11.2019.

Przybylski, Pamela (2011): Innovative Interaktionsstrukturen? Die Fernsehwirtschaft in der digitalen Welt, in: Wolling, Jens; Will, Andreas; Schumann, Christina (Hrsg.): Medieninnovationen – Wie Medienentwicklungen die Kommunikation in

Scholze-Stubenrecht, Werner et al. (2006): Duden: Die deutsche Rechtschreibung, 24. Aufl., Bd. 1, Mannheim: Dudenverlag, Bibliographisches Institut & F.A. Brockhaus.

Seufert, Wolfgang (2013a): Analyse des Einflusses von Veränderungen der Marktgröße, der Anbieterkonzentration und des Kostenniveaus auf das TV-Angebot in Deutschland, in: Seufert, Wolfgang; Sattelberger, Felix (Hrsg.): Langfristiger Wandel von Medienstrukturen – Theorien, Methoden, Befunde, in: Baden-Baden: Nomos Verlagsgesellschaft, S. 115–147.

Seufert, Wolfgang (2013b): Analyse des langfristigen Wandels von Medienstrukturen – theoretische Herausforderungen, in: Seufert, Wolfgang; Sattelberger, Felix (Hrsg.): Langfristiger Wandel von Medienstrukturen – Theorien, Methoden, Befunde, in: Baden-Baden: Nomos Verlagsgesellschaft, S. 7–30.

Shoutr Labs (2019): URL: https://shoutrlabs.com/, Abruf 08.11.2019.

Stückler, Moritz (20.04.2015): Live Krimi Spiel für Erwachsene, Wie die drei Fragezeichen, URL: http://www.spiegel.de/reise/europa/escape-the-room-raetsel-loesen-in-60-minuten-a-1028877.html, Abruf am 02.11.2019.

Thoma, Annette (05.04.2017a): Virtuelles Konzerthaus – Die AR-App „Konzerthaus Plus", URL: http://virtuelles-konzerthaus.de/ar-app-konzerthaus-plus/; Abruf am 02.11.2019.

Thoma, Annette: Neue AR-Postkarten im Konzerthaus Berlin (26.06.2017b), URL: http://virtuelles-konzerthaus.de/neue-ar-postkarten-im-konzerthaus-berlin/, Abruf am 02.11.2019.

Thoma, Annette: Klingende Karten: Das Virtuelle Quartett (04.06.2018), URL: http://virtuelles-konzerthaus.de/das-virtuelle-quartett/, Abruf 02.11.2019.

UFA (2019): Company URL: http://www.ufa.de/company/ufa/, Abruf am 26.09.2017.

UFA X (2019): Gateway to infinity. URL: http://www.ufa-x.de/gateway-to-infinity, Abruf am 20.01.2020.

Voigt, Kai-Ingo (2017): Gabler Wirtschaftslexikon Springer Gabler Verlag (Hrsg.): Gabler Wirtschaftslexikon, Stichwort: Produzent, URL: http://wirtschaftslexikon.gabler.de/Archiv/73891/produzent-v5.html, Abruf am 13.01.2020.

WDR (06.12.2016): WDR-Gesetz, URL: http://www1.wdr.de/unternehmen/der-wdr/profil/wdr-gesetz-102.pdf, Abruf am 13.01.2020.

WDR (2018a): Glückauf, URL: https://glueckauf.wdr.de/, Abruf 01.11.2019.

WDR (2018b): Zeitkapsel, URL: https://zeitkapsel.wdr.de/, Abruf 01.11.2019.

WDR (29.03.2019): AR 1933 – 1945 URL: https://www1.wdr.de/fernsehen/unterwegs-im-westen/ar-app/ar-app-info-100.html, Abruf 01.11.2019.

WDR (2019a): Dom360 – Der Kölner Dom – wie ihr ihn noch nicht erlebt habt, URL: http://dom360.wdr.de/, Abruf am 02.11.2019.

WDR(2019b): Dom360 – Geheimnisvolle Ecken, URL: http://dom360.wdr.de/geheimnisvolle-ecken/, Abruf am 02.11.2019.

WDR (2019c): Dom360 – Reise durch die Zeit, URL: http://dom360.wdr.de/reise-durch-die-zeit/, Abruf am 02.11.2019.

WDR (2019d): Dom360 – Hightech im Dom, URL: http://dom360.wdr.de/hightech-im-dom/, Abruf am 02.11.2019.

Analysis of the Expert Interviews

7

Companies that develop XR projects enter new territory and run the risk of failure. This sets innovation processes in motion within their own company that need to be managed.

This chapter evaluates the expert interviews in the five categories developed in Chapters 3–6.

The aim is to identify success factors via content-related, user-specific and production-related factors that enable the user to have a media-specific experience.

The analysis examines the producer level and the user level separately as there are different focal points. The producer level focuses on the framework conditions of production and innovation development in Category 3 (economy). At the user level, the content aspects and the user experience are examined for success factors in Categories 1 (content) and 2 (users). The learnings of the producers in Category 5 are directly assigned to the producer level and the user level and evaluated.

Differences between AR and VR are explicitly mentioned. The producers as well as the persons remain traceable in the quotations through their coding (see Appendix 1).

The analysis was carried out using a multi-stage text analysis. The basis of the following analysis is a final evaluation based on the four success factors (see Appendix 3).[1]

The success factors are used as abbreviations E1–E4 and described again in short form:

Success Factor 1 [E1]: "This has worked well or is standardized."
Success Factor 2 [E2]: "This worked particularly well and is special."
Success Factor 3 [E3]: "That was new or surprised the producer."

---

[1] Details of the assessment steps can be requested directly from the author by email.

Success Factor 4 [E4]: "That didn't work at all or is a risk."
The findings of the success factors are highlighted in bold in the text.

7.1   Success Factors at Producer Level

The following evaluation first examines the producer level of Category 3 (economy) using the subcategories. These include the team, the approach to production and the strategic-economic framework conditions. The findings are intended to provide information about which success factors contribute to taking user needs into account as early as the product development stage. This is important as it is assumed that a user-centred approach and specific framework conditions in the team and economy contribute to developing media-based innovations for AR and VR.

7.1.1   Team and Production

The teams of the nine producers are composed of different competences. Five of the producers presented have film expertise and thus the skills to develop and produce audiovisual content with the aim of satisfying needs through emotional and informative narrative forms (1/2/3/4/5). These competences are usually possessed by authors, editors, directors and producers. Content and thematic expertise is rated as particularly important by all producers as it is the prerequisite of content product development [E2][E3]. Three producers have game expertise in their team (5/6/7). Their competence is the satisfaction of the need for entertainment through dramaturgical interaction offers and user guidance via human–machine interfaces. This competence is rated as very high especially by producers with film expertise (1/2/3) [E2][E3]. For teams with a games focus, the desire for film experts is mentioned (6) [E3].

The competence to design spaces for VR and AR in product development is rated as particularly important by all nine producers [E2][E3]. Visual artists are present in five teams (2/3/4/5/7). Bringing in experts from outside the industry, such as architects or subject matter experts, is rated as an important finding (1/2/3/4/5/8) [E3]. Programmers are on the team at the three AR producers and the producers with a games focus (4/5/6/7/8) [E1]. For the other producers, programmers are brought in via research funding or on a project-by-project basis (1/2/3/9) [E1].

The teams' approach to product development differs in their methodological skills.[2] Consideration of user needs according to the four needs categories of the uses-and-gratification approach was used in a rudimentary way by one producer, starting from the

---

[2] The methods were not explicitly queried in the expert interviews in order to avoid manipulation. Therefore, no statement can be made about whether UX design was applied. In teams with programmers, this can be assumed (4/5/6/7/8).

goal of creating and rewarding special experiences for different needs through a story (1) [E2]. Other producers rate methods such as design thinking and a player-centred approach as very important as the user experience and need are at the heart of the development. The methods are applied in a standardized way to each of their developments (2/3/5/8) [E1] [E2]. "Game development is [...] a highly iterative process, [...] I prototype, get my test players, my target audience, try it out on them, evaluate that, then go back to development and tweak it incrementally, step by step, level by level until I get to the product, that is as good as it gets." (8B1) [E3] "In the process, the Vertical Slice³ is perfected in such a way that content can be easily transferred to subsequent missions." (8B2).

The visualization of 360° scenarios and individual perspectives in the development process is rated as particularly important (2) [E3]. "I would [...] try [...] to work much more visually in the next step. So to put the text even more in drawings [and] when we create an experience, then also think more of a spatial concept" (2B2) [3]. This statement refers to the storyboard of the film. One learning is to "make as broad a picture as possible in creating storyboards for 360° experiences" (2B1) [E3]. These methods have been found by producers [2/8] to be insufficiently evaluated for developing 360° user experiences for AR and VR [E4]. The challenge for all producers is to find new production processes that synchronize the 360° content and data sets, "it [is] a bit trial-and-error" (3B1) (1/2/3/6/9) [E3].

Discussing ideas in a team and making decisions in a team where no one has a claim to leadership (1/2/3/5/7/8) [E2] [E3] was rated as an important success factor. For some producers, this form of product development is used in a standardized way (2/3/5/8) [E1]. For others, the following new findings are important (1,5). "[...] In these discussions, results always came about that none of us could have brought about on our own. And that was the great discovery also for me, that a project in this complexity can also only be managed with a complex work process." (1B1) [E3] In this process, each team member is considered as a user. From this, development is free and without restriction. "You can do anything." (5B1) (1/2/5/7/8/9).

7.1.1.1 Interpretation

From the expert statements, three success factors can be identified for the subcategory team: **Multidisciplinary teams, user-related methodological expertise** and an **open discussion and decision-making culture.** The competencies of topic experts, film and game experts, and the competence of spatial 360° visualization were particularly emphasized. The involvement of further experts in the development process, such as outfitters and architects, is rated as an important success factor as this increases team competence.

Product development is an iterative process with many tests. Methods for identifying user needs and user guidance to integrate the user perspective already during development, as presented in Sects. 4.4, 5.1 and 5.2, form the second success factor. The insight of the

---

³ The Vertical Slice describes an agile process where the digital product's experience and added value is stringently considered at each level the user goes through (see Lawrence 27.06.2016).

producers is that these methods need to be further developed for the 360° perspective of the user. In addition, previous methods do not allow for a multi-dimensional 360° narrative. This makes it clear that the methods used are important, but not sufficient to integrate the 360° user perspective into project development. The inclusion of users in the development process is only used by one producer (2/8) [E2].

The third success factor is an open-ended creative and decision-making culture. Taking all team members into account and considering them as users brings new insights into potential user needs. In addition, the complex development processes can be distributed among several experts. As a positive finding, it was mentioned that no one has a claim to leadership and decisions are pitched and made in the team.

7.1.2 Economy and Market

The core business of most producers is in the media and creative industries. They produce cultural products (7/5) and media products (1/2/3/4). Producer 6 sees itself as a platform operator, producer 8 is a research institution, producer 9 manufactures aircraft engines. A total of six AR and VR projects (1/2/3/4/7/8/9) were funded through research budgets, grants from public funds, and fees. The budgets of the AR projects range from EUR 50,000 (4) to EUR 300,000 (7/8). The VR applications range from 500,000 EUR (1) to 1,000,000 EUR (2/3). Five of the knowledge and entertainment products are applied by users (1/4/5/7/9) [E2].

Producers 5 and 6 are start-ups whose holodecks are in the niche market of location-based VR entertainment. Their business model is to sell VR experiences based on VR adventures and games. Producer 5 already sells tickets for VR experiences as a group game and is the only one of the nine experts with a working business model with access to the user [E2]. Producer 6 is positioning itself as a location-based platform operator for VR content producers in the future.

AR and VR applications for knowledge transfer and location-based entertainment are said to have the highest market potential (1/3/5/6/8) [E2][E3]. It is seen as a problem that "media professionals and people who earn their money with it [...] if it comes up ten to 15 percent [...] have worn such glasses" [3B1]. Moreover, Moreover, content is something you have to stick with until it is done" (6B1) [E4]. For this, bold pioneers are needed. "If the experience [...] is better, more awesome, more exciting, more intense, more immersive, more profound [than] a movie, [...] then [users] are also willing to pay for the added value." (6B1) [E3].

On the other hand, producers are relaxed. "People don't perceive AR as a proposition yet. So you kind of don't have to worry about doing anything wrong." (4B1)[E3].

In industrial applications (9), the added value is demonstrated by faster decision-making processes. "We had a process where two departments had to agree [...] on some component, and that process, it used to take about three months, and they cut that down to ten minutes. [...] So the return on investment was achieved after one year." (9B1) [E3] (see para. 6.3.7).

VR and AR are seen as adding value to the industry. "To all the tech companies, I would advise them to roll that out right away because they already have the content. They just might not know it." (9B1).

Most producers consider an ecosystem consisting of content producers and an infrastructure of service providers to be a key success factor (2/3/4/5/6/7/8/9) [3]. This is justified by the need to establish a national location for VR and AR expertise vis-à-vis international competitors and to strengthen their own market position as the AR and VR market is viewed globally (2/3/4/5/6/7/9) [3].

7.1.2.1 Interpretation

These statements make it clear that the production of AR and VR applications are innovations for the producers. For Producers 6 and 7, the production of AR and VR is a radical innovation as they have not produced media productions before and need to acquire the skills in it. For the other producers, their products are incremental innovations as they build on their previous portfolio (1/2/3/4/5/8/9). The experts' statements also confirm that AR and VR media are at a very early stage of market differentiation (see Sects. 4.4 and 4.5). It is a risk for producers to invest in the development of applications as content production is the biggest cost factor. AR applications can be produced more cheaply as the 360° representation of space is a significant cost factor for VR. Seven out of nine applications were produced via research funding and grants. This indicates that experience still needs to be gained.

Accordingly, the success factors lie not only in the creation of user experiences, but also of producer experiences in the form of low-cost and low-risk production opportunities. Access to **funding opportunities** via subsidies and research funds can thus be identified as a success factor. At the market level, the success factors lie in the **entertainment, information** and **knowledge sectors** as it is evident that companies and users are willing to pay for the fulfilment of a need and knowledge transfer through AR and VR has a cost-efficient effect. **Sharing experiences** and knowledge forms another success factor. This is evident by the desire for an ecosystem to share production experiences and insights with each other. In addition, **data** is defined **as a success factor** to develop content for information and knowledge generation.

7.2   Overview of Success Factors Category 3

The Category 3 producer-level analysis identified seven success factors that favor the production of AR and VR applications.

The analysis confirms the assumption that AR and VR are innovation developments and require approaches that integrate the user perspective. The success factors identified were named by the producers as factors that, in their experience, favored the production process.

Table 7.1   Success factors Category 3 (Economy): Immersive Media Economy

Subcategories	Success factors
Team	Multidisciplinary teams
Production	Knowledge of methods
	Open discussion and decision-making culture without claim to leadership
Economics	Access to finance
Market potential	Information, knowledge transfer, entertainment
Ecosystem	Exchange and cooperation with competitors
	Access to data and users

Overview of success factors in Category 3 (Source: Own representation)

They provide a methodological approach to the production process and framework conditions. Since innovation is understood as a process, the application of these methods can have an influence on internal processes and structures at company level (see Sect. 4.3). In addition, framework conditions at the economic level are necessary in order to acquire skills through simple financing options and exchange and to reduce the production risk for media-based innovations for AR and VR. Access to data and users lays a foundation for business models. This has meant that producers are opening up to their competitors. In this respect, we can speak of the formation of an IMMERSIVE MEDIA ECONOMY (see Table 7.1).

7.3   Success Factors at User Level Content

The following analysis focuses on the user level. The analysis of success factors examines the content and the user experience. This should provide information about the content and design factors that are necessary to excite the user and which producers can apply to produce experiences. For this purpose the expert testimonies in Categories[4] 1 (content) and 2 (user experience) will be examined. Additional learnings from the producers are assigned to each of the categories.

7.3.1   Content and History

Content development is a standardized process for producers with film expertise (1/2/3/5). Starting with the story, the application is created. The next step is to determine the narrative. Technique and the format form the shell. The theme, story and narrative form thus define the media format (1/2/3/4/5) [E1]. The starting point for the story is sound content knowledge and the search for **powerful stories** to **tell concisely** (1/2/8) [E2]. Preliminary

---

[4]Category 1 includes the subcategories of content, story, space and interaction. Category 2 examines user needs based on reactions and user experience in terms of spatial and physical reactions during media use.

content research and access to **expert thematic knowledge** are considered factors for success (1/8) [E3]. Based on this novel narrative formats are developed. It has proven successful to link the content of the story directly to the virtual or virtually extended space (1/2/3/4/5/8) [E2]. **Linking story and space in terms of content** is judged to be a success factor (1/2/5/8) [E2]. The theme of time travel, into the future as well as into the past, is judged to be coherent for the medium and the content and a success factor for a story (1/2/5/8) [E3].

For this purpose a **narrative in episodes** was chosen. Each story is completed and tells only a part of the whole story. This arouses curiosity for the next episode (1/5/8) [E3]. **Arousing curiosity in the users,** offering them something to **discover or rediscover in the space,** is valued as a special insight. Several offers for different user types should be created (1/5/8) [E3]. Another insight is to make an **exclusive offer to** the user. Each story, each episode should provide the user with a **new experience** or **new insight.** These are basic criteria for content decision making (1/5/7/8) [E3]. For example, being allowed to sit next to the organ player in the cathedral to allow him to hear an organ concert by Charles-Marie Widor, which can be a **spiritual experience** for the user (1) [E3]. In AR and VR, a **story** is **experienced physically** (1/2/3/5/6/8) [E3]. Steering the user is described as a challenge, as a story is seen as guided (2/3) [E4].

Sensory stimuli can be used dramaturgically. They should be coherent with the story and the room. The sensory stimulus draws the **user's attention** to details, for example, a light goes on, something flies by or a sound is heard (2/5/8). This can be used to direct the story (2/8). This increases the **experience of presence or transportation** in AR and VR applications (1/5/6/8/9) [E3]. An important insight is to let the **user** become **part of the story** (2/3) [E3].

Basically, a narrative for VR and AR applications needs the narrative form of a children's film, "which tells the **becoming and the coming** along" (3B2) (1/3/5/6/8) [E3]. To achieve this, the producer must step back and **respectfully introduce** the user, less is more (1/3/5/6/7) [E3]. Simple **intuitive use** is recommended, so that even inexperienced users feel comfortable in the story and are not overwhelmed (1/2/3/5/6/7/8/9) [E3].

7.3.2   Space and Representation

The location is a uniform starting point for the story and the interaction (1/2/3/4/5/6/7/8/9) [E2]. The **fame, popularity and familiarity** of the content and spatial starting point, such as Cologne Cathedral and Roman Cologne, are rated as important criteria for **user willingness** to engage with the AR and VR application (1/8) [E2]. Spatial visualizations that the user is familiar with and associates with are rated highly. These are references to film quotes, as with the Escape Room (Metropolis) or Gateway To Infinity (Star Wars), or the familiarity of architectural styles (Art Deco), which establish a **link to the real place or a closeness to reality** (1/2/3/5/8) [E3]. The advantage of **visualizing architecture** and **historical life on site** was recognized (1/5/6/8/9) [E3].

Photorealistic representations are best received by the user because they are perceived as a film. CGI representations are classified as games. For the visualizations, original locations are suitable examples that are photographed, recombined and pre-visualized by visual artists (3/5) [E2]. **Acoustic stimuli make the spatial experience** in an AR and VR experience more natural and should be used more in the future (1/7/8) [E3].

The user is always confronted with the place. The real spatial experience must be taken as the **starting point for user perception** (1/2/3/5/6) [E3]. "And since we didn't do that, [...] then grown-up, strong, big guys [...] started to get all hectic with beads of sweat on their foreheads, because you noticed, oh, he's got a problem with depth now, [...] and a massive one. [...] because the brain is just not able to take metadata, information, but it is what it sees." (3B2) "[...] that's what I find quite amazing, that you can't use logic against it." (3B1) [E3] [E4] Also a **change of space** or **distance** must be smooth and comprehensible for the user, because the jumps in space are not yet learned experiences by the brain (1/2/3/5/6) [E4]. The introduction to the room, verbally in advance or as part of the story, as well as being escorted out, are rated as very important because the room is a new physical experience and the user first has to **orientate** himself in the **room** (1/2/3/5/6) [E3]. "Because that's the journey" (6B2).

Offering users exclusive places to which they otherwise have no access is assessed as a success factor (1/5/7/8) [E2]. These can be created through unique spatial experiences, such as hidden things or scenes or things that have disappeared, but are made visible again. (1/2/3/5/6/8/9) [E2].

7.3.2.1 Interaction Space

Interactions are offered to avoid frustration and boredom. The challenge is to find the right balance and the right offer for different types of users (1/5/6/7/8) [E3] [E4]. Each interaction should therefore **be simple** and lead to an **interesting outcome** that the user perceives as a **reward** (1/5/8) [E2]. For example, the reward can lead to a new thought, a new impression, or the discovery of a new piece of information that **helps the user move forward** (1,5,8) [E2].

Interaction with hands produces **higher presence experience** (1/2/3/5/6/7) [E2].

With regard to knowledge transfer, two spatial success factors are mentioned, firstly the realistic **three-dimensional size representation,** which makes more details visible. This leads to better understanding and knowledge transfer, which reduces the error rate (6/8/9) [E3]. The second success factor is the social component of **communication** in AR and VR applications. It promotes the team component and knowledge sharing and has a positive effect for collaborative learning, playing and constructing (5/6/8/9) [E3].

7.3.3 Interpretation

The expert statements make it clear that stories and content for VR and AR require different dramaturgies, narrative forms and stylistic devices than those previously used for films or games. The three-dimensionality of the space, the three-dimensional physical perception of the user and his presence in the space are part of the story and must always be taken into account.

The goal of producers is to create unique experiences that require the attention of the user. Attention forms the basis for the experience of presence and transportation (see Sect. 5.3). The creation of this user state is particularly intensive in AR and VR and is therefore a central success factor for AR and VR applications. In this respect we can speak of IMMERSIVE STORYTELLING in the production of AR and VR applications, the aim of which is to enhance the experience of presence and transportation. Unlike two-dimensional media, such as film, games or books, three-dimensionality must be taken into account in VR and AR. This requires stylistic devices and effects that contribute to the creation and enhancement of the experience of presence and transportation. According to the expert testimonies, the following criteria must be met for this: On the content level the story opens up an exclusive space for the users to have unique experiences, where they can make discoveries or rediscoveries in episodes to learn about things or themselves.

From the findings of the producers success factors can be identified that can be used for content implementation. These are derived from the analysis, with the aim of developing applications that provide a media-specific experience for the user. The content success factors are: **Uniqueness, Exclusivity, Adventures, Discoveries, Individual Experiences.** Considerations of these criteria favor the media experience and form the success factors for immersive storytelling of media-based innovations for AR and VR.

At the spatial level the success factors of **popularity, fame and familiarity of place** were identified based on the producer statements. The place is closely linked to the story and is shaped by natural sensory stimuli within which the users can physically move and interact. Through the users presence in the space, they become part of the place and the story. From the place they can overcome **space and time distances** and travel to new places through their own and simple interactions. The users are rewarded for their attention and willingness to interact. The reward principle shows an analogy with the uses-and-gratification approach. It can be assumed that Producer 1 has integrated the spatial user experience and interaction need in the development.

The criteria of **fame, familiarity, popularity, naturalness, simplicity** and **reward** form the success factors at the spatial and interaction level. The following success factors thus contribute positively to the experience of presence and transportation (see Table 7.2).

Accordingly, for immersive storytelling using AR and VR, stylistic devices and effects should be used that meet these criteria in order to stimulate the experience of presence and transportation in the user. The stylistic devices are, for example, sensory stimuli that guide the user through the story and the location and create a content-related sensory reference to the story and the location, episodic storytelling and genres that enable distance to be overcome. This enables an experience that the user can only experience through the media of AR and VR.

Table 7.2 Success factors Category 1 (content): immersive storytelling

Subcategories	Success factors
Content	Uniqueness, exclusivity
History	Discoveries, adventures
Subject	Individual experiences about something or oneself
Room	Fame, familiarity, popularity
Interaction	Overcoming distance
	Simplicity, natural sensory stimuli
	Reward

Overview of success factors in Category 1 (Source: Own representation)

7.4   Success Factors User Experience

The user level of Category 2 evaluates the success factors of the user experience based on user reactions observed by the producers that provide indications of needs.

7.4.1   User Reactions in General

User reactions to AR and VR applications vary. Users who are familiar with AR games like Pokémon Go show **quick adoption**. "They open the game and say, Ah this is like …" (8B2) With regards to AR-HisToGo, the game is also **fun for** adults. There is something for different types of players to discover, **entertainment** is the main focus (8) [E1]. For applications that require explanation, on the other hand, users need to be introduced, such as the dynamic music presentation in the season brochure of the AR app Konzerthaus Plus (7) [E4] (see Sect. 6.3.5).

VR applications elicit reactions ranging from "Nope, I don't want to play" (9B1) to reliable enthusiasm response after 5–10 s (1/5/6/9) [E3] [E4].

Basically, few users have experience with AR and VR. This is evident in how they use the media, "[like] a wooden person, like in cold water, just don't move, they look forward […] [that's] 360°-, but they look forward. They [don't] understand that that's not a TV." (7B1) [E4]. Experienced users move more confidently, know the 360° perspective and intuitively look for interaction offers (1/2/3/5/9) [E3].

AR and VR are basically associated **with games** by users, which is seen as a disadvantage by producers. The producers also mention that it is **difficult to convey** what happens in VR or in the CAVE (5/9) [E4]. For this, film comparisons are chosen that the user is familiar with. "So that's a 3D sequence that's going on there that you can interactively influence […] and walk through." (9B1) [E3] Many users want to make sure beforehand that they are not experiencing horror (5) [E3]. Producers **build trust through familiarity.** Older people can be introduced to VR well through a topic like architecture (5) [E2].

Afterwards, "they don't feel like they are playing a computer game now" (5B1). VR use and its acceptance are **not a question of age**, but a question of experience of use with these media (5/6) [E3].

7.4.2   Entertainment and Information Experience

The following user needs were explicitly named by the producers. A VR escape room experience is seen by users as an alternative to other events such as cinema, television or games. The users interviewed are male and female, young and older (5) [E2]. The expectation is that users want to be **entertained** (9) [E3].

The **well-being of** the user is seen as a central factor. According to the producers, users love **being in the VR** world and want to return to it. The perception of time is shortened (1/5/6) [E3]. In design processes, it is mentioned that after 10 min, engineers are **bubbling with ideas of** what can be done because they **recognize more** (9) [E3].

7.4.3   Interaction Experience

The historical time travel in VR, over which the user jumps into different times through his own interaction, "seems to overwhelm the user by giving him the illusion of [...] standing in front of the cathedral in the year 1600. [...] This experience, [...] which he triggers with this interaction, is apparently particularly intense in the episode Time Travel." This effect is also created in the AR app HisToGo. "So really standing in a place and rediscovering in life size, at least in a section, life as it was 2000 years ago, in this case [...]." (8B2) (1/8). The user's need for interaction is greater than previously assessed by the producers (1/2/3/5/7) [E3].

7.4.4   Spatial Experience and Bodily Experience

The user experiences in VR and AR with sensory stimuli such as acoustics and haptics are particularly intense and support the sense of space (6/7/8) [E2]. According to the findings of a producer, the virtual representation of a red, fluffy velvet wallpaper in a VR application leaves a realistically experienced sensory sensation when stroked, even though it is a woodchip wallpaper (6) [E3]. According to a study between the Technical University of Berlin, the University of Würzburg and Illusion Walk, perceptions and social behavior are linked to previous imprints (see Wienrich et al. 2018 p. 5 f.). These associated imprints or triggering by haptic stimuli, vibration, smells and wind recall memory images in the user, which, according to experts, are particularly intense in VR and are perceived as physical.

The intensity was measured in the study.[5] The user has a clear sense of space in VR and thus an **allocation** and **orientation** to things as in real physical space. This makes the **user feel present with his body in the medium** (5/6/8) [E2][E3].

Users who have a "volumetric experience for the first time, even with the depth, are totally flashed by this world, [but] don't get anything from the story" (2B2) [E3]. It is only on the second or third time that users are able to focus on the story and subtleties (2/3) [E3]. Reactions to the new spatial experience, for example, with depth and a spaceship passing by at the same time, overwhelmed some users. They have "ripped their glasses off their heads and said this is too much for me now. [...] People feel oppressed by it as if someone is entering their brain, generating images there and influencing them." (2/3) [E4].

The challenge is to create an event where the user says "I want to get in there too" (8B1) [E4]. The producers' insight is naturalness and "less is more" (3B2) when it comes to sensory stimuli (1/3/5/6/8) [E3].

The integration of the body in a VR and AR application is seen as a great "added value, [to] [...] move away from the cognitive and navigate an experience on another level as well, which may touch us differently and transform consequences from the game experience differently" (8B2) [E3]. The body as a place of learning and the spatial experience of three-dimensionality are evaluated as important cognitive factors of producers to be relearned and explored (2/3/6/8) [E3].

7.4.5   Avatars, Protagonists and Actors

In general, the integration and communication with real people in a virtual and virtually enhanced scene was rated positively. "You are always immersive in this scene, in the 3D scene." (9B1) The same view makes it easier to discuss problems. It is evaluated as more human, pleasant and natural (9) [E3].

The representation of real people in a VR application creates the illusion in the user that "yes, I am standing there in this place and I am part of this time travel" (1B1) [E3]. The character belongs to this scenery. The illusion is made even more surprising and powerful by the real person. "And I think the concept worked." (1B1) [E3] Users are surprised and look at the skin and texture of the clothes. Others keep a respectful distance from the actors. "That is, they perceive them as their counterparts [full persons]." (3B1) (1/2/3) Eye contact from the actor to the user in the virtual environment is described by the user as a "stark experience" (2B2) [E3]. The avatar is mentioned as a potential source of frustration as it does not interact with the user (5) [E4]. This deficit is made up for by dramaturgical elements (5) [E2].

---

[5] According to the expert (6B2), the subjects of the study had a clear memory of what they experienced, including a spatial one. According to the evaluation of the study, the users rated the feeling of being present in the virtual room positively by using a Likert scale with 9.5.

7.4.6   Interpretation of User Experience

The analysis of user experiences was based on expert testimonies that observed and reproduced user reactions during media use of AR and VR. These findings were evaluated to determine whether they provide indications of success factors that lead to a positive or negative user experience. A positive user experience is a prerequisite for willingness to engage with AR and VR media and turn attention to the content. This shift of attention creates presence experience and transportation and is thus the basic prerequisite for immersive storytelling.

User reactions show that AR and VR are generally associated with games. In addition, it is difficult to explain to new users what they experience in an AR and VR application. It was evaluated as a success factor that there is a basic curiosity and that users are enthusiastic after their first experiences with the media. The acceptance of use is independent of age.

Thus, familiarity of media use can be evaluated as a success factor and prerequisite that generates a positive basic attitude towards the media. Since the media are seen as an alternative to other media such as cinema, a need satisfaction for entertainment, information and knowledge is also associated with the media AR and VR. The observation that users want to return to this world, and time is perceived to be shortened supports the assumption. In addition, the observation indicates that the users feel physically and spatially comfortable and thus experience a high degree of presence in the medium and transportation.

Thus, **familiarity with** the medium, **physical and spatial comfort** with the medium, and **satisfaction of entertainment, knowledge** and **information needs** can be evaluated as success factors that an AR and VR application must meet in order for a user to feel comfortable.

Real people integrated into an AR and VR application are perceived as natural by the user. This promotes the experience of presence and the illusion of being in the story. It was particularly emphasized that users felt the need **to interact** with the actors. The desire for **autonomy of the interaction decision** seems to play an important role, such as approaching the actors or triggering the time travel itself. The own decision leads to a surprising adventure, to a new insight, to a new place, in a different time and provides the user with an **individual experience.**

The user experiences sensory stimuli directly. They influence his spatial and physical sensory perception. VR applications in particular trigger new sensory experiences for the user as he actually feels present in the media space. This media experience is positively experienced, as shown above, provided that the user feels comfortable. In this context, the desire for spatial and content-related security and orientation was observed, which requires accompanying the user into the medium and treating him or her with respect. This aspect is another success factor for the user to have a positive experience.

Accordingly, the desire for **self-determined interaction,** for an **individual experience** and for **novel physical and spatial sensory experiences** can be named as success factors for the fulfilment of user needs. These are supplemented by the desire for **integration** in

Table 7.3 Success factor Category 2 (users): immersive experience

Subcategories	Success factors
User needs	Familiarity with medium
General	Physical spatial Well-being
	Desire for entertainment, information and knowledge
Interaction	Self-determined interaction
Body	Individual experience
Room	Integration
	Novel body-space sensory experience
	Body as a place of learning
	Safety and orientation

Overview of success factors in Category 2 (Source: Own representation)

order to be a part of the experience, for **security** and the **possibility of orientation** as well as **familiarity of** media use and the desire for **entertainment, information** and **knowledge satisfaction.**

A particular insight of the producers is the physical experience of the users and the recognition of the **body as a place of learning and experience** in an AR and VR application. The fulfillment of these needs contribute to the well-being of the user, which leads to an increase in the experience of presence and transportation. In this respect we can speak of IMMERSIVE EXPERIENCE (see Table 7.3).

7.5   Conclusion of the Analysis of Success Factors

On the basis of the 14 expert statements it was possible to identify a total of 23 media-specific implementation criteria that favor the production of AR and VR experiences. At the producer level, seven success factors were derived from the statements that favor the development and production of successful content for AR and VR (see Sect. 7.1.2.1). At the user level, seven content-related criteria and nine user needs were derived that contribute to enhancing the user's presence experience and transportation and that enable a media-specific user experience. These criteria were combined into success factors and form the result of the analysis (see Sect. 7.3.1, Appendix 4 Overview of success factors for content production). An overview of the success factors identified can be found in Appendix 4 of this book.[6]

On the producer level in Category 3, the success factors are multidisciplinary teams and an open discussion and decision-making culture in the team as well as knowledge of user-centred methods. This confirms the assumption that methods that integrate user needs and

---

[6]The list of success factors provide a guide to producing AR and VR content. It can be downloaded as additional material at https://link.springer.com/book/10.1007/978-3-662-60825-8.

experiences and satisfy them, as presented in Sects. 5.1 and 5.2, can contribute to the development of innovative content productions.

High market potential for applications is seen in the knowledge, entertainment and information sectors. The economic success factors identified show that access to financing and funding helps to develop competencies for producing media innovations for AR and VR applications. In addition, the desire for exchange and cooperation between producers has been mentioned. For this producers need to open up to their competitors with the aim of jointly acquiring competencies and sharing the high costs of content production.

As the initial situation of the producers shows, access to the user is a central success factor for media economic business models (see Sect. 6.2). One finding of this work at the producer level is that involving users in the development process was used by only two producers (2/8). If producers were to involve users, information on specific user needs could be requested in addition to content aspects. This user-specific information provides indications of new offers and possible business models that producers can develop for themselves.

The success factors at the user level have identified content-related criteria according to which producers can implement user-oriented applications for AR and VR. The criteria focus on the special experiential value, exclusivity, and uniqueness of discoveries and experiences that can only be experienced through the immersive media AR and VR. The success factors familiarity, fame and popularity are aspects that positively influence the well-being of the user and thus the presence experience and transportation. In order to summarize these success factors in an umbrella term, the terms IMMERSIVE STORYTELLING and IMMERSIVE EXPERIENCES were developed. Neither term has a scientific definition. However, they refer to novel forms of storytelling that focus on enhancing the experience of presence and transporting the user. This paper offers a methodological approach to apply these terms in a practical way by considering the success factors in the three categories. Based on this, further stylistic devices for IMMERSIVE STORYTELLING and IMMERSIVE EXPERIENCES can be developed to produce applications for AR and VR that fulfill a user need and provide enrichment and reward for the user.

On the user experience side, the need for independent interaction and integration, as well as the desire for individual enrichment and experiences through novel sensory impressions, were identified. The consideration of physical-spatial user needs for safety, orientation and familiarity in a VR and AR application contributes to well-being, which leads to an increase in the user's experience of presence and transportation.

A particular insight of this thesis is the three-dimensionality of space and the associated spatial-physical experience of media use. This aspect was identified in the working definition on the basis of the characteristics of spatial perception and physical presence in the medium and theoretically derived as a media-specific assumption. Expert testimonies have confirmed this assumption (see Sect. 3.6.2).

In contrast to other media, the user's physical experience of entertainment and information is linked to a unique location. This represents a completely new form of media use

Table 7.4 Success factors for immersive storytelling and immersive experience

immersive storytelling	immersive experience
Uniqueness, exclusivity	Self-determined interaction
Discoveries, adventures	Novel physical and spatial sensory experience
Individual experience	Integration
Overcoming distance	Safety and orientation
Learn more about something or yourself	Physical Well-being
Familiar, well-known and popular	More natural, easier familiar access
Small physical challenges	Reward

Source: Own representation

that has the potential to create stories that can be experienced individually as the physical experience is unique to each user. The assumption can be derived from the expert observations. Based on the emotion and stimulation need, according to Green and Richter and the mood management theory, media use is an entertainment and excitement experience (see Sections 5.1.2 and 5.4.2.1). This need probably lies between the familiar and a challenge. The motive for media use with VR and AR would then be, for example, a fictional hero's journey, which the user undertakes in a self-determined and physical way. The physical media experience, enriched with sensory elements and real actors in a natural environment, would support the presence experience and transportation. Thus, as a finding for this work, **a pinch of physical challenge**, which can be experienced physically-sensually as an entertaining element of tension, can be added as a success factor.

Since every media use, as described in Sect. 5.1, serves to satisfy needs for which the user wants to be rewarded, the following reward promise for an immersive experience can be formulated on the basis of the identified success factors for VR and AR (see Table 7.4):

> You will experience a unique, exclusive surprising experience for your individual enrichment, through novel sensory experience in the form of your physically experienced hero's journey to extraordinary places, with extraordinary people who will inspire you and move you forward physically, sensually, intellectually and socially. This experience poses no danger to you. It enhances your well-being, is easily accessible, you can (share) it, and you will be rewarded for it. (Own definition based on success factors).

7.6   Challenges and Discussion

In addition to success factors, the analysis of success factors has also identified challenges that lie at the user and producer level. It becomes clear that the immersive media AR and VR have an image problem. The acceptance towards the media is low on both sides. On the user level, AR and VR are perceived as games. In addition, there is little experience of use, which emerges from the expert interviews (see Sect. 7.4.1). At the producer level, there is a lack of incentives to engage commercially with immersive media (see Sect. 7.1.2).

One approach to a solution is provided by Roger's diffusion theory, according to which targeted communication can help to increase acceptance (see Sect. 4.4). Here, for example, the special body-space experience and presence experience should be placed in the foreground. Involving different user types in product development would identify further user needs. Appropriate products can be developed on the basis of the needs identified.

This goal is being pursued by TV broadcasters such as WDR, for example, which has sufficient resources to produce VR and AR offerings and test them with users via its own channels. Producers need the same prerequisites. Interest groups from the media, commercial enterprises, producers and users would be one approach to developing projects collaboratively and distributing the production risk among several players. In this way, producers would have direct access to users and their data and feedback.

On the producer side of different industries, this would create incentives for further cooperation. This meets the producers' desire for a common ecosystem. Initial approaches to this can be seen in the founding of various associations in Germany and abroad in which companies, research institutions, media groups and start-ups are working together to establish and expand their own economy for immersive media (IMMERSIVE MEDIA ECONOMY), such as the First German Association for VR (see Erste Deutsche Fachverband für Virtual Reality 2019), the Visual Dimension Center (see Visual Dimension Center 2019) or the Virtual Reality Verein Berlin-Brandenburg or the VRARA Association, which has branches all over the world (see Virtual Reality Verein Berlin-Brandenburg 2018; VRARA Association 2019).

Economic framework conditions, such as an economically secured experimental space for the joint acquisition of expertise, are also suitable for developing an ecosystem and positioning oneself vis-à-vis international competitors. For this AR and VR producers need adapted economic funding that focuses on the promotion of novel content. This would help digitization in the media and creative industries. Hardware and software manufacturers would also benefit as they are dependent on content (see Sect. 1.1).

Another approach would be media-economic models that enable cooperation and collaboration for joint revenue generation. The prerequisite for this would be the opening of producers to their national competitors in order to share corporate knowledge. While this entails further changes in the media system at the actor, organizational and market level, this should be seen as an opportunity to avoid leaving the media market for AR and VR to international competitors (see Sects. 1.1 and 6.2). This would be one approach to forming the IMMERSIVE MEDIA ECONOMY. Such a project could be embedded in the framework of research on strategic innovation development processes.

In order to increase acceptance at the user level, communication about positive user experiences with AR and VR applications represents a central task. Experience-oriented communication, as used in brand communication or by TV broadcasters, could achieve positive emotionalization for VR and AR (see Esch et al. 2011, pp. 13–30). In it, for example, different user needs could be communicated, which the uses-and-gratifications approach offers (see Sect. 5.1). The challenge lies in describing the three-dimensional sensory body-space experience, since on the user side the three-dimensionality of media use has not yet been experienced. According to entertainment theory, it is assumed that a higher acceptance of content occurs when it is based on familiar narrative patterns (see Sect. 5.1.2). Analogies to other spatial-physical experiences such as architecture or sociology could provide an approach to this.

The methodical development for a three-dimensional media use for the development of a need category with integrated reward model is another central task. The methods presented, such as the uses-and-gratifications approach, UX design and design thinking, would then have to be adapted and further developed.

7.7   Conclusion and Criticism

This thesis aims to identify success factors for the content production of AR and VR products. For this purpose VR and AR were placed in the media context from a technological perspective and defined as immersive media. According to the working definition the dimensionality of space and user and the experience of presence are media-specific characteristics of AR and VR (see Sect. 3.6.2). The media context made it possible to analyse content-related, user-related and economic aspects of AR and VR. The reference to media innovations placed the focus of the investigation on user needs and the framework conditions of the producers.

On this basis five categories were developed, which form the basis for the investigation of the success factors. Based on interviews with experts, success factors in the categories of content, user and economy were identified. Based on the recognition of the three-dimensionality of spatial-physical media use, the terms IMMERSIVE STORYTELLING, IMMERSIVE EXPERIENCE and IMMERSIVE MEDIA ECONOMY were developed for the categories content, user and economy. These offer a methodical approach to enable producers to produce AR and VR applications that provide users with a three-dimensional media usage experience. It also helps producers to identify needs based on three-dimensionality in order to derive business models. The identified success factors for AR and VR content production are the result of the scientific investigation. They can be used as a guide and checklist by producers and downloaded from https://link.springer.com/book/10.1007/978-3-662-60825-8.

The theories selected for this thesis have enabled a media and communication studies approach to AR and VR. The research approach was chosen to be appropriately broad as basic findings about AR and VR as media innovations were to be identified. The exploratory approach has thus helped to gain a broad range of insights. At the same time the research has shown that, given the specific characteristics of AR and VR, the chosen theories and models are not sufficient. An investigation using the Sinus Milieu approach would have provided further insights into user types and their media use behaviour (see Flaig and Marc 2019). Building on this studies from motivation research, such as the limbic map, would be useful additions to gain deeper insights based on the motives for media use of AR and VR (see Häusel 2011, p. 52).

However, no clear user motives could be derived on the basis of the expert statements. This was also not queried in the interviews. The methodological approach has gaps in that the determination of success factors through the expert perspective only considered one perspective in a defined time frame. Although comprehensive information was obtained, it must be evaluated as a sample.

Only further development of the data and application of the results to concrete projects can confirm the accuracy of the findings. In addition, it must be examined whether these success factors can also be applied to projects outside of entertainment and knowledge transfer. In this context an application in brand communication would be an interesting approach.

It can nevertheless be stated that, on the basis of the choice of methods and the theories used, it was possible to develop initial findings on economic, content-related and user-related factors in relation to the media innovations AR and VR. Further investigations in the individual categories would deepen the knowledge gained.

Literature

Esch, Franz-Rudolf; Gawlowski, Domenika; Rühl, Vanessa (2011): Erlebnisorientiere Kommunikation sinnvoll gestalten und managen, in: Bauer, H.H., Heinrich, D., Samak, M. (Hsrg.): Erlebniskommunikation, Erfolgsfaktoren für Marketingpraxis, Berlin – Heidelberg: Springer Verlag.

Erster Deutscher Fachverband für Virtual Reality e. V. (2019), URL: edfvr.org, Abruf am 05.11.2019.

Flaig, Berthold-Bodo; Calmbach Marc (2019): Informationen zu den Sinus Milieus, Sinus Institut, URL: https://www.sinus-institut.de/veroeffentlichungen/downloads/, Abruf am 5.11.2019.

Häusel, Hans-Georg (2011): Die wissenschaftlich Fundierung des Limbic Ansatzes, URL: http://www.haeusel.com/wp-content/uploads/2016/03/wiss_fundierung_limbic_ansatz.pdf, Abruf am 05.11.2019.

Lawrence, Richard (27.06.2016): Vertical Slices and Scale, URL: http://agileforall.com/vertical-slices-and-scale/, Abruf am 05.11.2019.

VRARA Association (2019): URL: https://www.thevrara.com/, Abruf 08.11.2019.

Visual Dimension Center (VDC) (2019), URL: http://www.vdc-fellbach.de/, Abruf am 08.11.2019.

Virtual Reality Verein Berlin-Brandenburg (2018), URL: https://virtualrealitybb.org/, Abruf am 05.11.2019.

Wienrich, C. et al (2018): Social Presence and Cooperation in Large-Scale Multi-User Virtual Reality – The Relevance of Social Interdependence for Location-Based Environments, https://doi.org/10.1109/vr.2018.8446575.

Outlook

8

Those who deal with augmented and virtual reality today know the challenges of tomorrow.

This work shows that the immersive media AR and VR are used in all industries. It can therefore be assumed that AR and VR must be described as cross-sectional technologies. As in the case of digital media, the convergence of media can be observed through this cross-sectional technology, but also the softening of classic industry demarcations. At the same time a new industry is emerging (see Löffelholz and Thorsten 2003, p. 29; Beck 2003, pp. 79, 85; Sect. 1.1).

This presents producers and scientists with new economic and social challenges and requires changes on several levels. The changes lie in the formation of organizations and structures at the actor level – in order to network more closely with one another – as well as changes in a media economic system in which AR and VR producers can develop user-related business models.

A key success factor here is access to the user. This enables producers to personalize the immersive experience for the user on the basis of user data. Biometric data and emotional states can already be recorded via data glasses (see Hamilton 31.07.2017).

By controlling the user's emotions through eye tracking[1] or facial expression measurement through muscle contractions, the user can interact with figures in virtual space. This allows special experiences to be created, for example for a VR film (see Clay et al. 2019; Wolf 2019).

---

[1] Eye tracking is an established technique in psychological experiments. In combination with virtual reality, eye tracking enables better monitoring and control of human behavior under semi-realistic conditions.

In this way an AR or VR application could adapt to the emotional needs of the user, for example by manipulating the virtual (VR) and virtually augmented (AR) world with representations tailored to the user.

Assuming that access to users and their data is the prerequisite for successful digital business models, Google, Facebook and Co. have a significant market advantage. These companies are building their own VR and AR ecosystem by producing data glasses and building their own content platforms for VR and AR. Behind this lies the danger of international monopolization in the emerging market of the immersive media economy (see Sect. 1.1).

The primary goal of major digital companies is to digitize the world and obtain even more user data, for example through brain computing, a brain-machine interface that uses a person's neural system to use data to better control and optimize technology in hearing aids and prosthetics (see Debener and Dengler 2019). In the fall of 2019, Facebook bought the New York-based startup CTRL-Labs for US$500 million, which is working on a brain-computer interface (BCI) – designed to analyze and store human thoughts – to be able to control machines or robots through pure thought power (see Wagner 2019; Hoppenstedt 24.09.2019). This technology also enables new forms of communication and interaction in a VR and AR simulation, for example in social networks in a virtual reality platform where people meet and exchange ideas. Many companies worldwide are working on such social VR platforms (see G2 2019).[2]

The AR games Pokémon Go and Harry Potter: Wizards Unite by Google game producer Niantic are nothing more than global data collection machines. In 2018 alone, the company collected data from 150 million people worldwide with Pokémon Go. Research by journalists of the online platform Kotaku shows that Niantic documents and stores movement and behavioral data of its app users from around the world 13 times per minute through these games. At the same time players are deliberately sending local data to the company as this is part of the game. These are used to refine location tracking (see D'Anastiaso and Mehrotra 2019).

Whether it's brain computing for machine control or AR games for location tracking, these examples show that data collection is important on the one hand to improve products and develop new revenue models. On the other hand, data protection in a 360° digital media space, as in AR and VR applications, is not regulated, be it public or private.

The EU General Data Protection Regulation (GDPR) does regulate privacy rights for photos and video surveillance in both public and digital space. However, the collection of digital user data in a digital-public space is not regulated by the GDPR.

And current laws, such as the Media Act, do not apply because public space is not (yet) defined as digital-public media space.

However, the big digital companies such as Facebook, Microsoft, Apple and Google have long since measured the digital-public space with products and services and prepared

---

[2] For a recent overview of current social VR platform companies, visit G2 at https://www.g2.com/categories/vr-social-platforms, accessed 07/17/2022.

it economically. Their AR and VR experiences are offered as a complete package via closed ecosystems.

There is a lack of diversity for alternative AR and VR offerings, alternative platforms and technologies in the still young market. This diversity, and the low-threshold access to AR and VR offerings, are an important criterion for the differentiation process and the formation of the niche market for media innovations, which gives a creative developer scene and young industries room to develop (see Sect. 4.4, p. 5.2 f.).

Counter-movements such as initiatives and "open web" projects for VR and AR are steering against this, such as the US initiative "Immersive Web Community Group" and the – funded by the European Union – project "XR4All". Their goal is to develop a common standard for every Internet browser to make high-quality virtual reality and augmented reality projects accessible to everyone without barriers and easier for everyone to experience (see W3C 2019; XR4All 2019). However, in order to make an impact, they require equivalent conditions as digital corporations have. These are access to user data and research in biometric and geo-based data collection, brain-computer interface research and sufficient capital.

This outlook highlights a development that is already in full swing. This work therefore poses digital and data ethics questions about who will own sensitive user data in the future and what it will be used for.

At the same time this work would also like to encourage further thinking and research. Regulations and value models, in the form of business models, could contribute to a standardization process and thus to the establishment of AR and VR. They would be a relevant research approach to investigate the potential of a value-oriented IMMERSIVE MEDIA ECONOMY. A differentiated value attitude of VR and AR applications on the producer side could, for example, enable a differentiation strategy towards international market participants in order to offer specific user groups value-adapted AR and VR applications in the knowledge, information and entertainment sectors.

A joint research task of science and industry could, for example, be dedicated to the task of identifying user-specific needs and developing new types of offers and business models on this basis.

A methodological development of the concept of media that takes into account the body-space-media experience would also contribute to the identification of user needs in order to develop specific IMMERSIVE EXPERIENCES.

The further development of the definition of the 360° medium also stimulates a social discourse on data sovereignty in the context of user needs and the public space. This would be a multidisciplinary research task involving sociologists, architects, cognitive scientists, neurologists, sports scientists, physicians, media scientists, producers and business enterprises.

On the content level the narrative forms for IMMERSIVE STORYTELLING are far from exhausted. Investigations into the extent to which AR triggers transportation experiences for the user would offer further insights for market differentiation. One approach would be to create a narrative in public space with virtually enhanced elements in the backdrop of the real-physical environment on a specific topic.

In the process the human body – as a medium and place of individual knowledge acquisition – takes on a new meaning. Through the form in which new experiences are made through VR and AR, opportunities arise to find out something about oneself in a completely new way. Since humans are in a permanent reflection loop with themselves, they experience a different, new form of self-experience through the three-dimensionality of AR and VR. Behind this lies a new form of media use, with business models not yet developed. This outlook shows that AR and VR will significantly change media use and the world as we know it today.

8.1   Acknowledgement

This book would not have been written without the knowledge of the XR experts and their willingness to share their knowledge with me and to publish it. They are the ones who, with an investment of time and money, have made trend-setting experiences with the first XR projects in Germany, which have been compiled into the success factors in this book. My greatest thanks go to them. At this point the experts will no longer be mentioned by name as they are mentioned individually several times in the book (see Appendix 1).

I would also like to thank the many supporters, interlocutors and critics who supported me during the intensive examination of AR and VR and stood by my side during complicated processes. These are the professors Dr. Thomas Schildhauer and Dr. Georg-Dieter Adlmaier-Herbst and my fellow student Walter Kaul, who gave me valuable tips for writing the text. Above all, I would like to thank my friends, Bärbel and Kurt Sundermeyer for editing and Lucia Brauburger and Bruno Brunowski for always asking the right questions. Susanne and Peter Spielmann and Ute Stratemeier, who always got me out of my tunnel and invited me to concerts and to dinner. My thanks also go to my entire family, Helmut, Bruni, Irene, Peter P., the support of Peter K. and my wonderful children Maximilian and Paulina. Their encouragement, trust, deep conversations and wonderful distractions in everyday life, have given me the strength to write this scientific paper. I would also like to take this opportunity to thank my project manager Martin Börger and his team at Springer Vieweg Verlag, who had confidence in me and made this publication possible. If I have not mentioned anyone here, she and he deserve just as much appreciation and gratitude as those mentioned.

Literature

Beck, Klaus (2003): Neue Medien – neue Theorie? in: Löffelholz, Martin; Quandt, Thorsten (Hrsg.), Die neue Kommunikationswissenschaft. Theorien, Themen und Berufsfelder im Internet-Zeitalter. Eine Einführung. Wiesbaden: Westdeutscher Verlag, S. 71–87.

Clay, Viviane, König; Peter, Koenig; Sabine (2019): Eye Tracking in Virtual Reality, Journal of Eye Movement Research. 12. https://doi.org/10.16910/jemr.12.1.3., Abruf 08.11.2019.

D'Anastiaso, Ceciloa; Mehrotra, Dhruv (16.10.2019) The Creators Of Pokémon Go Mapped The World. Now They're Mapping You, Kotaku, URL: https://kotaku.com/the-creators-of-pokemon-go-mapped-the-world-now-theyre-1838974714, Abruf am 08.11.2019.

Debener, Stefan; Dengler, Reinhard (2019): Task Group 7: Brain-Computer Interface für Hörhilfen; Berlin Brain-Computer Interface, URL: https://hearing4all.eu/DE/Forschung/C/Task-Group-7.php, Abruf 08.11.2019.

Hamilton, Ian (31.07.2017): SIGGRAPH 2017: Neurable Lets You Control A Virtual World With Your Mind, UploadVR, URL: https://uploadvr.com/siggraph-neurable-lets-control-virtual-world-thought/, Abruf am 08.11.2019.

Hoppenstedt, Max (24.9.2019): Brain-Computer-Interfaces:Facebook greift nach den Gedanken, Süddeutsche Zeitung, URL: https://www.sueddeutsche.de/digital/brain-computer-interface-facebook-ctrl-labs-1.4614663, Abruf am 08.11.2019.

Löffelholz, Martin; Quandt Thorsten (2003): Kommunikationswissenschaften im Wandel, in: Löffelholz, Martin; Quandt, Thorsten (Hrsg.): Die neue Kommunikationswissenschaft. Theorien, Themen und Berufsfelder im Internet-Zeitalter, Eine Einführung, Wiesbaden: Westdeutscher Verlag, S. 13–42.

Wagner, Kurt (2019): Facebook to Buy Startup for Controlling Comuter With Your Mind, Bloomberg, URL: https://www.bloomberg.com/news/articles/2019-09-23/facebook-to-buy-startup-for-controlling-computers-with-your-mind, Abruf 29.09.2019.

Wolf, Claudia (2019): Affektive-Flexibilitaet, Methods Berlin, URL: http://methods-berlin.com/de/affektive-flexibilitaet-studieninformationen/, Abruf am 08.11.2019.

W3C (2019): Community & Business Groups, URL: https://www.w3.org/community/immersive-web/,ABruf 09.11.2019.

XR4All (2019): Moving the European XR tech industry forward, URL: http://xr4all.eu/, Abruf am 09.11.2019.

Appendix

A.1. Annex 1

Overview of the experts with codes

	Industry	Project	Description
A)	**Media industry**		
1 (1B1)	**WDR** **Thomas Hallet** Project Manager	"360Dom.com" Virtual reality project as interactive CGI production with 360° videos	Thomas Hallet initiated and supervised the entire project with 5 WDR internal colleagues and external employees. In the VR application users experience the Cologne Cathedral through content offerings such as 360° videos, flying through the cathedral and other interaction options.
2 (2B1) (2B2)	**UFA Lab** **Floris Ash** Story creation **Daniel Brückner** Project management	"Gateway To Infinity" virtual reality CGI and 3D human body reconstruction (3D HBR) with two actors, walk-through cinema film	Daniel Brückner and Floris Asche wrote the story and implemented it dramaturgically and in terms of content. In the sci-fi scenario the user stands on a rock in front of a cave entrance and watches two real actors guarding the gate to eternity. The user can get close to the actors.
3 (3B1) (3B2)	**UFA Serial** **Drama** **Frank Govaere** CGI /VFX creation **Ernst Feiler** Production Manager UFA		As head of production at UFA, Ernst Feiler is interested in building a technical infrastructure for novel technologies and integrating them into UFA's workflow. Frank Govaere is an expert for visual and special effects (VFX) at UFA and was responsible for the VR room design.

(*continued*)

© The Author(s), under exclusive license to Springer-Verlag GmbH, DE, part of Springer Nature 2023
E. Langer, *Media Innovations AR and VR*,
https://doi.org/10.1007/978-3-662-66280-9

(continued)

	Industry	Project	Description
Overview of the experts with codes			
4 (4B1)	**Miriquidi Film** **Michael Geidel** Managing Director and Project Manager AR Contents	"Pastors' kids" Augmented reality project for museum knowledge transfer	Michael Geidel is managing director and produces film and TV movies, transmedia projects, gaming and 3D VR movies. The company is based in Munich, Leipzig and Potsdam. The AR project "Pfarrerskinder" was developed as a supplement to the travelling exhibition as part of the Reformation anniversary for "Luther Year 2017".
B)	**Holodeck/ Entertainment**		
5 (5B1)	**EXIT VR** **Sven Häberlein** Managing Director Project Manager Creation	"Huxley" virtual reality project as location-based Escape Room Game	Sven Häberlein is co-founder of the startup Exit VR, which operates an Escape Room. Groups of players go through a VR application in a team and have to try to get out of the room using playful elements.
6 (6B1) (6B2)	**Illusion Walk** **Jim Rüggeberg** Managing Director **Andrea Heuck** Project Manager Science	"Immersive desk" VR CGI production for training and entertainment	Jim Rüggeberg and his brother Julien developed a walk-through holodeck in 2013. The user enters an off-shore platform in the VR goggles, to which he has to come up himself with an elevator in order to make repairs up there. The holodeck was developed for training and games and can integrate any content, such as walk-in showrooms or films.
C)	**Concert hall**		
7 (7B1) (7B2)	**Concert House Berlin** **Albrecht Sensch** Project Manager Technology **Annette Thoma** Project Manager Music	"Concert House Plus AR App" for knowledge transfer classical music	The Berlin Konzerthaus hosts 600 classical music concerts. The AR project Konzerthaus Plus is part of the project "The Virtual Concert Hall" with the goal to convey classical music in a new way. Albrecht Sensch is responsible for the implementation as technical director. Annette Thoma is responsible for the musicological side.
D)	**Science**		

(*continued*)

(continued)

Overview of the experts with codes			
	Industry	Project	Description
8 (8B1) (8B2)	**Cologne Games Lab** **Dr. Björn Bartholdy** Co-director and Head Games Research **Katharina Tillmanns** VR & AR Games Research and Research Director HisToGo	"HisToGo" AR App knowledge transfer game	Dr. Björn Bartholdy is co-director of the Cologne Games Lab, which is located at the TH Köln and is responsible for the development of new research projects, among other things. The research project HisToGo is an AR game for historical knowledge transfer. Research director is Katharina Tillmanns.
E)	**Industry**		
9 (9B1)	**Rolls Royce** **Dr. Marius Swoboda** Project Manager	Product "Development mixed reality" CAVE with interactive CGI production	To improve product development, the British engine manufacturer Rolls Royce has built a CAVE that allows engineers to work collaboratively in teams and at different locations. Dr. Marius Swoboda developed the project as head of Rolls Royce's internal department for human-machine design research together with the Universität Cottbus and installed it at Rolls Royce.

Overview of the producers for the expert interviews (Own representation)

A.2. Annex 2

Overview categories for expert interview		
Categories	Subcategories	Aspects
Content **User level**	Media format	Technology Purpose Approach
	Stories and content	Form of dramaturgy Three-dimensionality content Special features of the content
	Space and interaction	Three-dimensionality space Representation of media integration Interaction space, three-dimensionality
	Approach user needs	Consideration of user needs, media use and target group

(continued)

(continued)

Overview categories for expert interview		
Categories	Subcategories	Aspects
Users **User level**	User reactions Media usage	Adventure, individual experience, Reactions in general
	User experience Entertainment and information	Motivation for entertainment, Information, communication
	Interaction and communication experience	Application as a group, alone with objects
	Space and body experience	Three-dimensional spatial perception Movement, presence experience Body Experience Sensory stimuli
	Experience with avatars/actors/ protagonists	Communication and interaction with protagonists/actors/colleagues
Economics **Producer level**	Team	Competence External competence and partners
	Production	Costs, time Approach, management Financial framework
	Market potential	Added value for companies Identifiable user needs Business models and clients
	Ecosystem	Partner, exchange, cooperation, collaboration
Producer **Producer level**	Initial situation and motivation	Previous experience In-house development, research project Task/objective Market leadership
Learnings **Producer and user level**	Personal insights Advantages, disadvantages AR and VR Assessment according to strengths and weaknesses Other	Assessments according to important findings in the previous categories and personal insights

Overview of the categories for expert interviews (Own representation)

A.3. Annex 3

Evaluation criteria of the success factors

Success factor 1 [E1]: "This has worked well or is standardized."

In success factor 1, approaches are assigned that are based on standardized and previous processes and do not represent novelties, but have proven themselves from the producer's perspective.

Success factor 2 [E2]: **"This worked particularly well and is special."**

New approaches and non-standardized processes are evaluated as success factor 2. These are, for example, the integration of existing solutions from other areas or own solutions that have worked particularly well.

Success factor 3 [E3]: **"That was new or surprised the producer."**

In success factor 3 statements and approaches are assigned that have a high degree of innovation and were particularly successful. This also includes important and surprising insights of the producer, which are adopted for the next productions.

Success factor 4 [E4]: **"That did not work at all or is a risk."**

Statements indicating that something was very difficult or did not resonate with the user are assigned to this success factor. The producers' findings about negative factors are taken into account, as these point to hurdles and challenges that need to be considered and solved.

A.4. Annex 4

Overview of success factors for media-based innovations

Success factors category 1 (content) Immersive storytelling	
Subcategories	**Success factors**
Content **History** **Subject**	Uniqueness, exclusivity Discoveries, experiences Individual experiences about something or oneself
Room **Interaction**	Familiarity, Fame, Popularity Overcoming distance Simplicity, natural sensory stimuli Reward
Success factors category 2 (users) Immersive experience	
Subcategories	**Success factors**
User requirements **General**	Familiarity with medium Physical spatial well-being Desire for entertainment, information and knowledge
Interaction **Body** **Room** **Hero's journey**	Self-determined interaction Individual experience Integration Novel body-space sensory experience Body as a place of learning Safety and orientation A bit of physical challenge

(continued)

(continued)

Success factors category 3 (economy) Immersive media economy	
Subcategories	**Success factors**
Team	Multidisciplinary teams
Production	Knowledge of methods
	Open discussion and decision-making culture without claim to leadership
Economics	Access to finance
Market potential	Information, knowledge transfer, entertainment
Ecosystem	Exchange and cooperation with competitors
	Access to data and users

Overview of success factors for media-based innovations

Printed in the United States
by Baker & Taylor Publisher Services